Letters
from
Korean
History

Notes on the English translation

Korean personal names, place names, proper nouns and common nouns have been transliterated according to the Revised Romanization of Korean system, introduced by the South Korean government in 2000. The only exceptions are names that are widely recognized in other forms, such as Syngman Rhee (Lee Seungman) or Kim Ilsung (Kim Ilseong). Two of the most common Korean surnames, Kim and Park, have been left in their conventional forms, rather than Gim and Bak (which would be their spellings according to the Revised Romanization system). The surname Lee, meanwhile, is transliterated as Yi before 1945, in accordance with convention (for example, Yi Seonggye), and then in the more modern form of Lee after 1945, taking Korean liberation as a somewhat arbitrary dividing line. Surnames are listed before first names, in the Korean style, with the singular, Americanized exception of Syngman Rhee.

The ages of individuals are listed in accordance with the original Korean text of *Letters from Korean History*, which naturally follows the Korean convention for age calculation. This means that figures given are generally one year higher than what would be considered the corresponding "Western" age.

Letters
from
Korean
History

1

From prehistory to Unified Silla and Balhae

Park Eunbong

CUM LIBRO 책과함께

History in Northeast Asia is like a minefield. Riddled with unresolved issues, controversies, disputed territory and conflicting ideologies, it often breeds acrimony among governments and peoples in the region. Within many countries, too, blind nationalism, political bias and censorship constantly threaten to distort the picture painted by historians of their country's past and, by extension, present. Creating a balanced narrative in the midst of such tension and conflicting perspectives is no easy task. But that is what Park Eunbong appears to have done in *Letters from Korean History*.

Offering children and young readers an unbiased version of their past is one of the kindest and most responsible ways of helping them grow into broad-minded citizens, capable of sustaining peace and cooperation in a region - and world - that grows more interconnected every year but still bears unhealed historical scars and bruises. In Korea, such a history also offers context that can put the country's current state of division - only sixty-seven years old as of 2015 - into wider perspective.

Making any Korean book accessible to readers of English through translation is a privilege. The same goes for *Letters from Korean History*. In a series of letters addressed to a young reader overseas, the author adopts a conversational style of writing that conveys the ups and downs, ins and outs of Korean history with ease. But while the language is highly accessible, the content is never rendered simplistic or patronizing, and issues that lose some other historians in a fog of

nationalism are navigated by Park with the kind of healthy detachment and clarity that inspires confidence in the reader.

Progressing from the stones and bones of prehistory all the way to the turbulent twentieth century in the course of five volumes, *Letters from Korean History* can be browsed as a reference text or plowed through from beginning to end. As with most histories that cover such a long period, the density of information increases as the narrative approaches the present. The relatively recent Joseon period, for example, accounts for two of the five volumes (III and IV), rich as it is in events and meticulously recorded historical data.

Letters from Korean History has been a great success in its native country among Korean readers. I hope that this translation will now be of help to ethnic Koreans overseas, others interested in Korea or history in general, Koreans looking to study history and English at the same time, and anybody else who believes that exploring the past is a good way to try and make sense of the confusing, flawed and wonderful present.

Ben Jackson
May, 2016

To readers of 'Letters from Korean History'

Letters from Korean History is a series of some seventy letters covering a period that stretches from prehistory to the present. Unlike most introductions to Korean history, it takes a theme-based approach: each theme functions as a window onto a particular period. The use of several different windows offering various perspectives onto the same period is meant to help the reader form her or his own more complete picture of that part of history. For example, "Buddhism, key to the culture of the Three Kingdoms" and "Silla, land of the bone-rank system," two letters in Volume I, offer two different ways of understanding Silla history: a religious perspective via Buddhism; and a social caste-based perspective by way of the bone-rank system. My hope is that, after reading both letters and exploring these two separate approaches, readers will come closer to gaining a comprehensive understanding of Silla. The more diverse the windows opened, the more helpful this should be in the forming of a complete image.

Letters from Korean History places equal emphasis on aspects such as culture, everyday life, society and social segments with habitually low historical profiles, such as women and children. This is an important difference to conventional introductory histories, which naturally tend towards narratives centered on ruling classes by prioritizing political history.

I have also attempted to portray Korean history not as that of a single nation in isolation but as part of world history as a whole, and to adopt a perspective that places humans as just one species in the universe and nature. This is why the first letter begins not with prehistory on the Korean Peninsula but with the birth of the human race on Earth. The connection with world history is maintained throughout the five volumes, in which Korea's interactions, relationships and

points of comparison with the rest of the world are constantly explored.

The single most distinct aspect of *Letters from Korean History* is that, unlike most general histories, which make passing references to characters and dates, it depicts Korea's past through a series of engaging stories. It is my hope that these will help readers feel like direct witnesses to historical scenes as they unfold. All content is based on historical materials, either in their original form or adapted without distortion. Sources include key texts such as *Samguk sagi* ("History of the Three Kingdoms"), *Samguk yusa* ("Memorabilia of the Three Kingdoms"), Goryeosa ("History of Goryeo") and *Joseon wangjo sillok* ("Royal Annals of the Joseon Dynasty"), as well as a variety of literary anthologies, letters, journals and epigraphs.

The English version of *Letters from Korean History* is published for young readers overseas who are curious about Korea and its people, and for young Korean readers keen to learn more about their own history while improving their language skills as global citizens. I hope that readers will not feel obliged to start at the beginning of Volume I and plow all the way through; rather, each letter contains a historical episode in its own right, and can be chosen and read according to the reader's particular area of interest. The text is complemented by plenty of photos and illustrations, giving a more vivid sense of history - reading the captions that accompany these should enhance the sense of historical exploration.

I very much hope that this book will become a useful source of guidance for young readers, wherever they may be.

Park Eunbong

May, 2016

Contents

CHAPTER 1

When did the first humans settle in Korea?

Caves made comfortable homes. Their inhabitants must have gathered there and sat down for a tasty dinner each evening when the sun went down. Whatever food had been brought back was shared. Nobody tried to hog anything just because they had provided it themselves. Since finding food was such a tough job, sharing it all out equally was the only way of making sure those that hadn't found any didn't starve.

| TIME LINE |  | | |

C. 700000 B.C. ⸱⸱⸱⸱⸱⸱⸱⸱⸱ **C. 8000 B.C.** ⸱⸱⸱⸱⸱⸱⸱⸱⸱ **C. 2300 B.C.** ⸱⸱⸱⸱⸱⸱⸱⸱⸱

Paleolithic period
Stone tools

Neolithic period
Earthenware made from
clay; agriculture begins

Gojoseon founded
Dangun Wanggeom
foundation myth

You may wonder if prehistoric people lived on the Korean Peninsula.

Of course they did. There were dinosaurs, too. If you go to what's now Goseong in the province of Gyeongsangnam-do, you'll find plenty of dinosaur footprints.

Last time we talked about prehistoric people for hours; today, I'm going to tell you some more.

People have lived on the Korean Peninsula for a very long time. How long? About 700,000 years. That's far enough back to make a family tree taller than you could ever imagine. By then, though, the dinosaurs had all disappeared. People came onto the scene only once dinosaurs were extinct.

While the prehistoric period, by definition, provides us with no written sources, we have another way of learning about the distant past: nature. We can read the mountains, seas, rivers, rocks and other natural elements around us like living books. Human remains and artifacts hidden deep in caves, fossils concealed within ancient rocks, tracks buried in the ground - these are the things that can teach us about prehistory today.

Well then - let's go on a journey to see what prehistoric secrets nature holds.

C. 1000 B.C.	C. 400 B.C.	C. 37 B.C.	427
Bronze Age	**Iron Age**	**Goguryeo founded**	**Goguryeo**
Bronze swords and mirrors	Iron weapons and farming implements	Jumong establishes Goguryeo at Jolbon	Capital moved to Pyeongyang

When did humans first appear on earth? Around four million years ago. Some scholars claim five million years; others still, seven million. Such differing opinions reflect the difficulty of finding and interpreting material that holds information about the prehistoric era.

Four million years is a hard length of time to imagine. Think of the age of earth, though: around 4.6 billion years old. In terms of global history, then, the appearance of people is quite a recent event.

And what did the first people look like? Monkeys? Well, yes. Unlike people today, they did look a bit like monkeys. Since then, with the passing of time, we've gradually evolved to look the way we do today. The very first people had to pass several milestones on the long road to becoming modern humans.

Walking on two legs:

the first step to becoming human

The first landmark in human evolution was the transition from walking on four legs to using only two. Our distant ancestors moved about on four legs, like other animals. So what made them stand up to walk?

Scientists offer several different explanations. Some say it was in order to free up two hands for other uses; others point out that walking on two legs is a much more efficient way of using energy. Whatever the answer, what's clear is that walking on two legs was more suitable than four when it came to adapting to different environments.

As you know, our distant ancestors had nothing as useful as the powerful claws of other beasts or the wings of birds. They weren't particularly big or strong, either.

Holding no particular advantage over other animals, wouldn't these creatures have needed something more if they were to avoid starving or falling prey to other beasts? Perhaps the transition to two feet was a reflection of this necessity. And this became their first step on the path to becoming humans like us.

The second milestone: taming fire

Another critical juncture in the evolution of humans was mastering the use of fire. Once they had learned to use fire to their advantage, humans were no longer animals at all.

At first, fire must have been scary. How terrifying must it have been when lightning lit up the night sky, followed by deafening bursts of thunder? Faced with a rapidly spreading forest fire, early humans must have turned and fled.

People walk on two feet
Once people began walking upright, they found themselves with two free hands. By standing, walking and running on two feet, they were able to find the food they needed.

One day, somebody realized that fire was not just scary but warm, too. A few brave and curious individuals must have carefully carried a burning branch into the cave, Just to warm up on a cold night.

Another advantage of fire was the security it offered by keeping other animals, who still feared it, at bay. It became

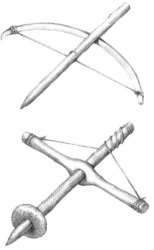

Bow drills
Bow drills such as these were used to light fires. When a piece of very hard wood and a piece of soft wood rub against each other for a long time, the resulting friction ends up creating fire. The use of fire brought huge progress to people's lives. It was a highly valuable commodity - and a frightening one if misused. Managing fire properly was very important.

clear that fire, when used the right way, was really not a bad thing at all. People found ways of keeping fires going, so that the embers never died completely. And ways of lighting new fires when they did go out.

Oh - and they also realized that meat, which they had previously only eaten raw, was absolutely delicious when

Hand axe
This multifunctional tool was a favorite in the Paleolithic period. It was used for cutting meat and digging the ground.
–Institute of Cultural Properties, Hanyang University

Pick
Picks were smaller than hand axes and had sharpened tips. They were sometimes used as spears, with handles attached.

cooked on a fire. And easier to digest. This was something discovered by chance, when somebody happened to eat the flesh of a burned animal. From then on, people would go scavenging after forest fires in search of cooked meat.

According to archaeological evidence gathered so far, people began using fire around 400,000 to 500,000 years ago. Which means they spent the first 3.5 million years or so after appearing on Earth eating raw meat and trembling on pitch-black, cold nights just like other animals.

Two free hands

The third important milestone was the use of tools. Having begun walking on two feet, humans now began using their two spare front feet - we'd better call them hands from now on - to make and use tools. Monkeys, of course, know how to use tools too. You must have seen them taking sticks to knock down fruit from high up in trees. What they can't do, however, is make tools for specific purposes. But humans now could.

People picked up stones and either used them as they were or broke them into forms for specific uses. Later, they began making polished stone implements.

The period when this happened is known

as the "Stone Age" and can be broadly divided into the Paleolithic and Neolithic periods. Let's start by having a look at the former.

Paleolithic cave dwellers

The Paleolithic period lasted from the time people first began using stone tools, an unimaginable 2.5 million years back, to around 10,000 years ago.

Important Paleolithic sites on the Korean Peninsula include Mt. Seungnisan Cave in Deokcheon, Pyeongannam-do Province; Mandal-ri in Pyeongyang; Geomeunmoru Cave in Sangwon; Seokjang-ri in Gongju, Chungcheongnam-do; Jeongok-ri in Yeoncheon, Gyeonggi-do; and Geumgul Cave in Danyang, Chungcheongbuk-do. Sometimes it feels strange to think that we live in the same places these people did several hundreds of thousands of years ago.

The most problematic issue in the Paleolithic era was getting enough food. If you enjoy eating and hate being hungry, you'll understand how they felt.

How did they go about feeding themselves at a time when there were no shops or markets?

Paleolithic people obtained their food from the areas around their caves. Still unable to build houses

Scraper
Made by shaping fragments of broken rock, sharp scrapers such as these were used like knives when skinning animals.
–Cheongju National Museum

Chopping tool
Made by chipping away one or both sides of a large pebble, this tool was used for stripping off rough tree bark. –Institute of Cultural Properties, Hanyang University

Paleolithic sites on the Korean Peninsula

Jongseong
Unggi
Mt. Baekdusan
Deokcheon
EAST SEA
Sangwon
Pyeongyang
Yeoncheon
Paju
YELLOW SEA
Danyang · Jecheon
Cheongwon
Gongju
Suncheon

Geumgul Cave
This cave is located in Danyang, Chungcheongbuk-do Province and was lived in by cavemen. Can you see the entrance? It looks small from the outside but is surprisingly big once you go in. The cave is more than eighty meters long. Its inhabitants would have gathered food nearby.

of their own, they made use of shelters provided by nature. Of course, not all Paleolithic people, throughout their millions of years of existence, lived only in caves. Some of them lived by rivers, lakes or the sea, and some on hills. But since most of them did live in caves, we generally describe them as cavemen.

A few years ago, I visited a cave in Danyang, Chung-cheongbuk-do Province, that had been inhabited in Paleolithic times. Located halfway up a mountain, it had a small entrance and was so inconspicuous that you would barely have spotted it from the outside. On the inside, though, it was quite spacious and offered a good view of the surrounding area to anyone crouching down and looking out.

Hunting and gathering in the Paleolithic period
Paleolithic people hunted in groups. While men went off further away, women stayed closer to home, gathering food. They picked fruit from the trees and dug roots from the ground.

The people who lived in this cave would have got up with the sunrise and gone looking for food in the surrounding mountains. They gathered anything edible they could get their hands on: fruit and berries from the trees, grasses, roots and crayfish from the local streams. This is why they were known as "gatherers."

But gathering was not as easy as it sounds. Anyone picking poison mushrooms or getting bitten by a snake would quickly be in big trouble. Because of this, gatherers went around in groups, led by whoever had the most experience and knew the woods best.

Were these people vegetarians? No: they also ate the meat of animals they had hunted. You might imagine them as brave warriors, fighting ferocious beasts, but it seems people did not take on wild animals to start with. The weapons they had weren't up to much, and they themselves were weak. Rather, they probably scavenged for carcasses left from the kills of other animals.

Does that disappoint you? Gradually, though, people developed weapons such as arrows and began hunting for themselves. The stone arrowheads you'll have seen in various museums are exactly the kind of things they used for hunting.

Paleolithic people did not hunt or eat meat all that

Upper jawbone of a cave bear (above) and lower jawbone of a large Merck's rhinoceros (below) The cave bear and large Merck's rhinoceros made good game but are extinct today. These bones were discovered at Geomeunmoru Cave in Sangwon and Mt. Seungnisan Cave in Deokcheon, respectively.

often. Hunting was hard work. On a normal day, they ate fruit and other gathered food; meat was eaten on festive occasions. Their youngsters, especially, must have counted down the days to the next time they'd eat meat. Maybe you do the same - who knows?

Community and equality at dinner time

Caves made comfortable homes. Their inhabitants must have gathered there and sat down for a tasty dinner each evening when the sun went down. Whatever food had been brought back was shared. Nobody tried to hog anything just because they had prvided it themselves. Since finding food was such

Distinguishing between eras based on tools

Over the years, humans have made tools from various materials: stone, bronze, iron, wood, animal bone, and so on. In the 19th century, a Danish architect and museum director named Christian Jürgensen Thomsen was pondering ways of organizing and classifying antiquities for display. Eventually, he decided to distinguish between a Stone Age, a Bronze Age and an Iron Age, according to the tools used in each. Later, an Englishman by the name of John Lubbock divided the Stone Age once again, into two periods: the Paleolithic, followed by the Neolithic.

This system is still widely used across the world today. Means of distinguishing between eras can be as varied as you like. But I think I'll follow this one. Until I find a better one, that is.

Altamira cave paintings
The depiction of these
bison in red and black is
so lifelike that they seem
about jump into action.
These Paleolithic wall
paintings were found in the
Cave of Altamira, near the
town of Santillana del Mar
in northern Spain, by a little
girl who was exploring the
cave with her father.

a tough job, sharing it all out equally was the only way of making sure those that hadn't it found any didn't starve.

If people kept on dying, the community as a whole would be weakened, making survival more difficult. This is why scientists claim the Paleolithic period was one of egalitarian, communal life.

Later at night, when all the children were asleep, the adults would have looked up at the sky outside the cave, with its torrents of stars and its moon that changed shape every night...

People in those days were much more in touch with nature than we are. Art comes from those whose hearts and minds are close to nature. Paleolithic people created paintings on the walls of their caves and carved beautiful sculptures from animal bones. This was the period that gave us the paintings in the Cave of Altamira in Spain and the bone carvings found at Jeommal Cave in Jecheon, Chungcheongbuk-do Province.

As they painted and carved, they must have made their own silent wishes: "I hope the coming hunt goes well." ... "I hope the new cave we're moving to is bigger than this one."

People in the Paleolithic period couldn't live in the same cave for very long. After sweeping up everything there was to eat nearby, they had to move on in search of more food. They therefore spent their lives wandering from place to place.

Did they have families like ours in those days? Scientists have various opinions regarding this question. Some believe there were no nuclear families like those of today, and that communities of several dozen people raised children born among them communally, with no couples of the sort we know. Others claim that there were families based on children born to recognized couples back then, too. What do you think?

What did Paleolithic Koreans look like?

The Korean Peninsula was inhabited from early on. Paleolithic artifacts and remains have been discovered in several places here. Human bones are also sometimes found at Paleolithic sites. By carefully putting them back together, we can have some idea of how these people looked. Let's take a look at some reconstructed Paleolithic faces.

What do you think? Are they anything like Koreans today? Are we descended from Paleolithic people? Some say yes, but the general view is that our ancestors emerged in the Neolithic period.

'Yeokpo Girl'
A young girl whose remains were discovered at Yeokpo-ri in Pyeongyang

Reconstructions of Paleolithic people

Paleolithic bone sites on the Korean Peninsula

Mt. Seungnisan cave, Deokcheon

Yeokpo-ri, Pyeongyang

Mandal-ri, Pyeongyang

Heungsugul cave, Cheongwon

Mt. Seungnisan Man
Remains discovered at Mt. Seungnisan Cave in Deokcheon-gun, Pyeongannam-do Province.

'Mandal Man'
Remains discovered at Mandal-ri, Pyeongyang

'Heungsu Boy'
Discovered at Heungsugul Cave in Cheongwon, Chungcheongbuk-do Province –Chungbuk National University Museum

CHAPTER 2

How did Neolithic Koreans live?

Who do you think would come out higher in an IQ test: a Neolithic youth or you? Would you be scared to see the result?

People in the Neolithic period were no less intelligent than we are today. Their brains were almost the same size as ours. That's why scientists say there's no guarantee that our IQs are any higher than theirs. Be careful about calling them "primitive" - you might end up looking stupid yourself.

C.700000 B.C.

Paleolithic period
Stone tools

C. 8000 B.C.

Neolithic period
Earthenware made from
clay; agriculture begins

C. 2300 B.C.

Gojoseon founded
Dangun Wanggeom
foundation myth

Around 10,000 years ago, Earth's atmosphere underwent a dramatic change. The Ice Age came to an end and the weather grew warmer. As ice melted in the north, rivers and seas rose. Low-lying areas of land were flooded.

As the Yellow Sea and the Korea Strait formed, Korea, which had been part of the same huge landmass as China and Japan, became the peninsula it is today.

People began adapting to their new environment. The wisdom they had built up over millions of years now began to come into its own.

They started making better, more useful tools. Before, they had simply used chipped pieces of stone; now, they began shaping tools into sophisticated shapes for specific uses. These are known as polished stone tools. They also created vessels for storing food, made of clay baked into earthenware.

This age of polished stone implements and earthenware is known as the Neolithic period. In Korea, it began around 8,000 years ago.

Well then - let's have a look at how people lived during the Neolithic period.

C. 1000 B.C.	C. 400 B.C.	C. 37 B.C.	427
Bronze Age	**Iron Age**	**Goguryeo founded**	**Goguryeo**
Bronze swords and mirrors	Iron weapons and farming implements	Jumong establishes Goguryeo at Jolbon	Capital moved to Pyeongyang

Who do you think would come out higher in an IQ test: a Neolithic youth or you? Would you be scared to see the result?

People in the Neolithic period were no less intelligent than we are today. Their brains were almost the same size as ours. That's why scientists say there's no guarantee that our IQs are any higher than theirs. Be careful about calling them "primitive" - you might end up looking stupid yourself.

Fishing net weights and hooks
Attaching stone weights to fishing nets allowed them to be properly centered, making them much easier to use. The photo at the top shows a reconstruction of a net with weights attached. Fishing hooks were generally made of animal bones.

–Gwangju National Museum

–National Museum of Korea

Life by the river and on the beach

Have you been to Amsa-dong, near the banks of the Hangang River in Seoul? It's the site of a Neolithic village.

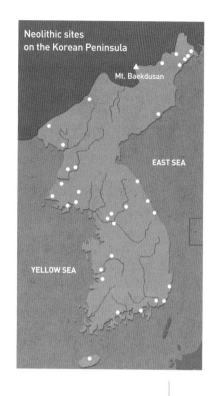

Neolithic sites on the Korean Peninsula

Mt. Baekdusan

EAST SEA

YELLOW SEA

Neolithic people lived together in communities like this, generally situated on riverbanks, by the sea or on islands.

Water is a rich source of food. The fish and shellfish that arrived as the climate grew warmer were rich in nutrients and tasted delicious. If you want to catch fish, though, you need the right tools. So people invented harpoons, fishhooks and nets.

Neolithic people ate as much fish and shellfish as they liked. Fish bones and scales found at a shell midden in Dongsam-dong, Busan, show that they ate a lot of snapper, Spanish mackerel, shark and sea urchin. They also enjoyed oysters, abalone, conches and freshwater snails.

The warm weather and abundant water allowed new plants to grow in the forests. The fish in the water, meanwhile, were practically inexhaustible in their abundance. There was more to eat than before, and life became a lot easier.

The Neolithic diet was much more plentiful than that of the Paleolithic period. Fish, shellfish, venison from deer hunts, all sorts of fruits, nuts and grasses...

What's more, as I've just mentioned, Neolithic people were the first to practice agriculture. This meant that cereals were another part of their diet, so they

Spindle whorls
Spindle whorls like this were used to spin thread when a rod was placed through the hole in their center, attached to a bundle of fibre, and spun around.

- Buyeo National Museum

must have been a lot better nourished than their Paleolithic forebears.

Cooking methods and implements also developed. Neolithic people boiled water and flour from cereals in earthenware vessels to make porridge. They also made things similar to the *tteok* (rice cakes) that people eat in Korea today.

Earthenware items were used for storing grain and for cooking. The Neolithic period is best known for its comb-pattern pottery. How on earth do you think people stood pots with conical bases? Apparently they buried them in the ground or carried them around in net bags like the ones we use for watermelons today.

You will remember how people in the Paleolithic period wore leather clothes made from animal hides. In the Neolithic period, however, they extracted thread from plants and used it to make fabric.

Thread was drawn from hemp plants. The outer skin was peeled off and the white inner skin split into narrow strips; this was then twisted into long threads using a spindle. By weaving these threads to produce fabric, and sewing pieces of it together using bone needles, Neolithic people were able to produce beautiful dresses and other pieces of clothing.

That's not all: Neolithic people decorated themselves as

Comb-pattern earthenware
This type of earthenware is characterized by the distinctive patterns that give it its name. Why did people carve patterns on earthenware? Some scholars say it was to make it look good; others say it was to stop it cracking or breaking during firing.
–National Museum of Korea

Replica of rock carvings at Bangudae, Ulsan
The face of this huge rock, some eight meters long by two meters high, is full of carvings. Let's see what they depict: whales, turtles, dogs, deer, wild boar, animals trapped inside nets or fences, a boat with several people in it, and even some human faces. Some scholars say the carvings date from the Neolithic period; others place them in the Bronze Age. In any case, they were clearly created over a long period of time.
– Gyeongju National Museum

Accessories
These accessories include bracelets made of seashell and a necklace and anklet made of animal teeth. Another seashell has been shaped to look like a human face.
– National Museum of Korea

much as possible with seashell bracelets and necklaces, and animal fang anklets. Both women and men wore accessories like these, which also functioned as good luck charms. Who knows? - Perhaps they put them on when they went hunting, to pray for a good catch.

Neolithic people also caught whales. At Ulju in Ulsan is a huge rock, covered in prehistoric carvings, known as Bangudae. Among the turtles, deer, wild boar and hunters, amazingly, are dozens of whales. You'll also find pictures of boats that appear to have been used for catching whales.

The sea came right

up to today's Ulsan a few thousand years ago, so it looks as if the people of Bangudae took boats down the Taehwagang River on whale hunts. As you gaze at the carvings on the rock, you can almost hear the songs of those brave whale hunters way back then.

Stone arrowheads (reproduction)
Arrowheads such as these were used for hunting, an activity that continued from the Paleolithic into the Neolithic period.
–Jeju National Museum

Dugout homes

Unlike their Paleolithic forebears, who lived in natural caves, Neolithic people knew how to build their own homes.

They began by digging pits in the ground and putting up strong wooden poles, then made roofs from straw or grass. Their homes were something like a semi-basement flat today. If you've ever been in a basement on a cold day, you'll know that it's much warmer than outside. And much cooler than outside in summer. Neolithic people made use of this principle: for them, it was a natural heating and cooling system.

A house like this is known as a dugout. From the outside, it looks like a huge

Dugouts at Amsa-dong Prehistoric Settlement Site
Located in modern Seoul's Amsa-dong neighborhood, this was the site of Neolithic dwellings. The dugout homes that now stand here are recent reproductions. Neolithic people generally lived by water; Amsa-dong, too, is close to the Hangang River.

Site of Neolithic homes
This site is located in Amsa-dong in Seoul. You can see the remain of a fireplaces.

conical hat. Inside, it has a fireplace towards the center of the floor where food is cooked. Lighting fires here also provides heating.

Tools such as stone knives, axes and arrowheads were kept near the entrance to the dugout, making them easy to pick up on the way out to work or hunt. Earthenware vessels for storing food were kept further inside.

A typical dugout housed four or five people: a nuclear family similar to those we have today. Life in their small but cozy single-roomed dugout must have been happy and intimate.

Dugout life
Here, we see a mother lighting a fire in the fireplace and a father preparing some game for the cooking pot. In the corner, a child seems to be practicing making stone weapons. It looks as if he'll be going with his father on the next hunting trip, taking the weapon he has made himself. Through the doorway, you can see people building another dugout in the distance.

The dawn of agriculture

Among all the achievements of the Neolithic period, agriculture is surely the greatest. While gathering, hunting and fishing involve taking food provided by nature itself, agriculture is about humans applying their own strength to nature to produce what they eat. So how did people come to start farming? Probably when somebody saw how the seeds from discarded fruit sprouted, grew and bore more fruit, put two and two together and realized that planting seeds would bring more food.

Farming first began on Earth around 10,000 years ago. This was probably around the time it started in Korea, too.

It's difficult to pinpoint any single reason why people starting farming after picking wild fruit and hunting animals for millions of years. Some say it was an attempt to adapt to a new environment after warmer weather caused animals to migrate elsewhere and meat became scarce. Others say it was because population growth meant that old methods were no longer sufficient to feed everyone, and that agriculture offered the chance to produce lots of food on a small amount of land and a guaranteed return on the work invested.

Agriculture dramatically changed the course of human history. In the

Stone plowshare
This plowshare was attached to a long stick and used to turn over the earth.
−Hanyang University Museum

Bone pick
Made from a bifurcated animal horn, this tool was used for weeding and making holes to sow seeds.

Neolithic period, people gradually began living in the same place for longer. They started farming, which gave them even less need to wander around in search of food. And wherever they planted seeds, they had to settle and wait until harvest time. This is what we now call sedentary life.

Neolithic people also began raising livestock, keeping animals in manmade enclosures rather than simply hunting and killing them in the wild. Some animals were killed when humans were ready to eat them; others were tamed and used for hunting or to bear burdens.

The first animal to be raised by humans was the dog. Man's new best friend played the star role in every hunting trip, running ahead to chase the quarry. Pigs came next. Cows, widely used in agriculture, were raised only much later on.

Agriculture
The farmers here are using a stone plowshare to turn the soil and a horn pick to make holes for sowing seeds. Early farmers sowed crops including various types of millet and sorghum. Rice cultivation only began much later. Most Neolithic people had no idea what rice tasted like.

Exhibition model, Amsa-dong Prehistoric Settlement Site
This model depicts the life of Neolithic people, hard at work outside their dugouts.

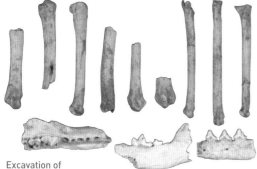

Excavation of Neolithic dog bones
A complete set of dog bones- skull, jawbones, vertebrae and all- were found on Daeyeonpyeong-do Island off the west coast of Korea. This tells us that Neolithic people were already raising dogs 6,000 years ago.
−National Research Institute of Cultural Heritage

The emergence of inequality

Like that of the Paleolithic period before it, Neolithic society was equal. Soon, however, an important transformation began: the relationships between previously equal people were changing. At first, agriculture produced relatively low yields and required labour from many people, so that all the inhabitants of each village worked together and divided the harvest equally. As time passed, however, farming techniques and tools gradually developed and food become more plentiful. Agriculture no longer required the efforts of the entire village, and families could produce more than enough food through their own work alone. The food surplus grew steadily greater.

Neolithic people now faced the new problem of what to do with all the leftover food they produced. It was no longer the communal property of the whole village; instead, it gradually moved into the possession of single families or individuals. Communities came to have rich and poor member, and differences in status began to emerge. Relationships became unequal.

The Neolithic agricultural revolution

All the changes that began with agriculture are collectively known as the "agricultural revolution," just as the transformation brought to our lives today by computers is sometimes called the "information revolution." One thing is worth bearing in mind here: despite the use of the word "revolution," these changes did not take place all at once. People didn't just suddenly abandon their previous way of life and turn exclusively to farming. Rather, they carried on gathering, hunting and fishing long after agriculture first emerged. The shift took place little by little, over an extended period of time.

Pestle and ground stone
Utensils such as these were used for removing the shells or skins of hard fruits and nuts by grinding. With the advent of agriculture, they were also used for separating grain from its husks.
–Chuncheon National Museum

Stone tools

You will recall how people in the Stone Age used either chipped or polished stone implements. The transition from the former to the latter reflected the accumulation of knowledge. People found it inconvenient to use crude chipped stone tools and started polishing them on other, smoother stones. They gave their tools sharp blades and refined them so that they were easier to use, according to their designated purposes. The change from chipped to polished implements is not simply about the development of tools: it also signifies the transition from the Paleolithic to the Neolithic period.

Let's have a look at how Stone Age people made their tools.

Chipped stone tools
–Institute of Cultural Properties, Hanyang University

Polished stone tools
–National Museum of Korea

• Ways of making a chipped stone tool --

Anvil chipping
Break the work piece on a large anvil stone, then use the resulting fragment as it is.

Direct chipping
Hold the work piece and a hammering stone in each hand and chip the former directly with the latter.

Indirect chipping
Rather than hitting the work piece directly with a hammering stone, use a chisel made from bone or horn.

Pressure chipping
Scrape the work piece into shape by applying pressure using a tool smaller and sharper than a hammering stone.

• Ways of making a polished stone tool --------------------- ----------

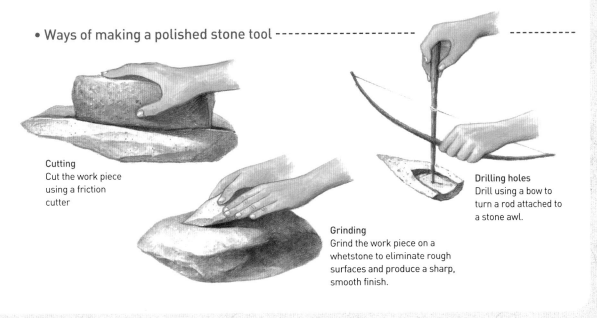

Cutting
Cut the work piece using a friction cutter

Drilling holes
Drill using a bow to turn a rod attached to a stone awl.

Grinding
Grind the work piece on a whetstone to eliminate rough surfaces and produce a sharp, smooth finish.

CHAPTER 3

The Bronze Age
and Gojoseon,
the first state
in Korean history

You may have heard the story of Dangun Wanggeom, which tells how a very patient she-bear was transformed into a woman who married Hwanung - son of Hwanin, the king of heaven - and gave birth to Dangun. Dangun, so the story goes, went on to found the state of Gojoseon.

"What kind of bear turns into a human?" you're probably thinking. "Nonsense. It has to be fiction."

Taken word for word, of course, it's pretty unbelievable. But this is a story we must interpret symbolically if any sense is to be made of it.

C. 700000 B.C.

C. 8000 B.C.

C. 2300 B.C.

Paleolithic period
Stone tools

Neolithic period
Earthenware made from clay; agriculture begins

Gojoseon founded
Dangun Wanggeom foundation myth

These days, some people get absorbed in computer games like Age of Empires - I've caught a glimpse of them myself and they're very interesting. You start with a few simple thatched huts in a clearing in the woods, then get more and more land, gather food, build up strength, win territory through endless wars with neighboring villages and eventually found a whole state. Long ago, of course, all of these things really did go on. Around 3,000 BC, various civilizations began appearing around the world. This generally happened in areas next to large rivers, with abundant, fertile farmland. The Four Great ancient civilizations are prime examples of this. In these regions, cities appeared, writing systems were created, and states, ruled by kings, came into being. Surely something similar would have been happening around this time on and around the Korean Peninsula. Wouldn't the people here, after centuries of farming, settled life and gradual development, have naturally become ready to establish a state?

The first state in Korean history was Gojoseon. Let's have a look at how it was established.

You will recall how I mentioned that, towards the end of the Neolithic period, the accumulation of surplus food resulted in the emergence of a rich-poor divide. The egalitarian societies that had existed, uninterrupted, since humans first appeared on the planet several million years earlier, were plunged into crisis. These circumstances produced powerful rulers: individuals who were good fighters, won the respect of others through their wisdom, or had accumulated the most assets.

Rulers led their people into wars with neighboring villages. These conflicts were started for several reasons, usually in order to seize some precious asset or other or to grab farmland.

Dolmen at Bugeun-ri, Ganghwa-do Island
Dolmens were a key form of Bronze Age tomb. There are around 150 on the island of Ganghwa-do. The dolmen in the Ganghwa-do village of Bugeon-ri is taller than a full-grown person. How could people have built such big structures?

Bronze daggers
Early bronze daggers were shaped like a *bipa* (a mandolin-like instrument) and therefore called "*bipa* swords (left)." Many of these have been discovered in the Liaoning region of Manchuria. They were later replaced by slender daggers, which have only been discovered on the Korean Peninsula (right).
–Buyeo National Museum
–National Museum of Korea

Bronze dagger moulds
Moulds such as these were used for casting daggers, allowing multiple items of the same form to be created. Moulds were generally made of stone.
–Buyeo National Museum

The people of the defeated village would be taken to work as slaves for their conquerors, further increasing the latters' wealth and power.

Bronze implements: atomic bombs of their age

When a Bronze Age village went to war, its ruler would take along a bronze sword. Made from an alloy of copper and tin, bronze swords were incomparably harder, sharper and more beautiful than stone blades. Bronze implements like this symbolized the enormous power of rulers. That's why some scholars now say that possessing bronze weapons was, at the time, like being armed with nuclear weapons today.

No matter how you look at it, the transition from stone to bronze seems miraculous. Who knows - maybe someone exceptionally curious and observant stumbled on the idea of making bronze after seeing molten lava cool into hard rock after a volcanic eruption.

Copper and tin mined in the mountains were melted over a strong fire, then poured into a mould to make bronze ware - a technique immeasurably more demanding and difficult than anything used to make stone implements. Now, only certain people with specialist skills were able to make tools. This era,

• Forging Bronze

Copper and tin were placed in a crucible and melted over a hot fire.

The resulting molten alloy was poured into a mould.

Next, the forged piece of bronze was left to cool and then trimmed into its final shape.

At last, it was ready.

Ruler with bronze mirror and bells
At rites, a ruler would appear in front of his people wearing a bronze mirror and bronze bells. The mirror would catch and reflect the sunlight, making the ruler as dazzling as the sun itself.
– Jeonju National Museum

too, is now named after the material it used: the Bronze Age. In Korea, it started around the 10th century BC.

Though the Bronze Age had begun, farming implements were not cast from the new metal but still made of stone. Rather, bronze was used to make weapons, ritual vessels, mirrors, bells, buttons, and accessories such as rings. Tools that needed to be sharp, such as chisels and gimlets, were also made of bronze.

Bronze mirrors were originally made not for practical purposes but as accessories for rulers. They would hang mirrors around their necks, take bronze swords and bells, gather their people and conduct rituals. The round mirror represented the sun; the sunlight it reflected must have made its wearer appear as brilliant as the sun itself and elevated his status accordingly.

It was in the Bronze Age that the first states appeared. The story of Dangun Wanggeom, which is told in the early Korean history book *Samguk*

Bronze bells and mirrors
Items such as these were used by rulers as accessories and utensils for rites.

yusa, ("Memorabilia of the Three Kingdoms") is set in the Bronze Age. Let's have a look at Gojoseon, the first state in Korean history.

Gojoseon

You may have heard the story of Dangun Wanggeom, which tells of how a very patient she-bear was transformed into a woman who married Hwanung - son of Hwanin, the king of heaven - and gave birth to Dangun. Dangun, so the story goes, went on to found the state of Gojoseon.

"What kind of bear turns into a human?" you're probably thinking. "Nonsense. It has to be fiction."

Taken word for word, of course, it's pretty unbelievable. But this is a story we must interpret symbolically if any sense is to be made of it.

Many countries and peoples around the world have their own founding myths involving distant ancestors. Some are said to have come down from heaven; others to be directly descended from the gods. The foundation myth of ancient Rome tells how Romulus, eventual founder of the city, and his twin brother Remus are born as the sons of Mars, the god of war, abandoned on the banks of the Tiber and rescued by a she-wolf who raises them as her own.

Myths are hard to believe when taken literally, but they do

Saw-tooth axe
This Bronze Age stone axe is believed to have been placed on the end of a pole and used during rites by a ruler to direct proceedings, rather than as a practical tool.

Romulus and Remus
The two protagonists of the foundation myth of the Roman Empire are said to have been suckled and raised by a she-wolf.

contain the thoughts and emotions of those who have valued and preserved them over the years. Searching for the facts and meanings hidden in these mysterious stories is one way of studying history. The story of Dangun Wanggeom, like the foundation myths of other countries, contains clues as to the lifestyle, thoughts and feelings of Korean ancestors. Let's take a closer look into it.

What the Dangun Wanggeom story tells us

The Dangun Wanggeom foundation myth has reached us in its current form after having been passed down by word of mouth over many generations. In this process, various elements have been added and changed.

The story tells us several things about the lives people led at the time Gojoseon was founded. Given the huge influence that weather exerts on agriculture, the fact that Hwanung was accompanied by rulers of wind, rain and clouds tells us how important farming was at the time.

The claim that Hwanung came down from Heaven, meanwhile, indicates that he appeared as a new ruler, or as the representative of a new ruling group. Such myths often use the concepts of Heaven or man to represent groups

Samguk yusa ('Memorabillia of the Three kingdoms')
The Buddhist monk Iryeon wrote this history, in approximately 1281 during the Goryeo period. Today, it is the oldest surviving text to contain the story of Dangun Wanggeom.

that arrive from elsewhere, and the concepts of Earth or woman to represent the group already living in the region in question. In Greek myth, too, Zeus was the god of a people that had migrated from elsewhere, while his wife, Hera, was the goddess of one that had originally inhabited the region in question.

The marriage between the bear-woman and Hwanung signifies the integration of the two groups. And the fact that

The story of Dangun Wanggeom, founder of Gojoseon

Dangun Wanggeom

Long ago, Hwanung, the son of Hwanin, King of Heaven, longed to rule over the world of humans. When he learned of the will of his son, Hwanin looked down from Heaven and chose Mt. Taebaeksan as a suitable seat of government. He gave Hwanung three heavenly seals and sent him down to rule. The heavenly prince led an entourage of 3,000 followers down to a sacred tree on the summit of the mountain, a place that he named Sinsi. He is often referred to as "Heavenly King Hwanung." Commanding the spirits of wind, rain and clouds as his ministers, he presided over some 360 aspects of human life, including grain, punishment and the determination of good and evil. At that time, there were a bear and a tiger living together in a cave, both of whom pleaded with Hwanung to make them into humans. He gave them mugwort and garlic, saying:

"If you eat these for 100 days while staying out of the sunlight, you'll become human."

The tiger was unable to bear these conditions, but the bear endured them and, after twenty-one days, became a woman. She married Hwanung and bore him a son: Dangun Wanggeom. The boy went on to build a capital at Asadal and found a state, which he named Joseon. –From Samguk yusa

Bear and tiger depicted in a Goguryeo tomb mural
People at this time belonged to groups, each of which worshipped a special animal of its own such as the bear, the tiger or the bird. This practice is known as totemism. It appears the story of Dangun Wanggeom, which features a bear and a tiger, was passed on from Gojoseon to the later state of Goguryeo. This Goguryeo tomb mural shows two people wrestling; in the background, though the picture has been partly lost and is hard to make out, are a bear and a tiger crouching under a huge tree.

the tiger was unable to endure the ordeal in the cave but the bear managed to stick it out and ended up marrying Hwanung indicates that a people that worshipped the bear integrated with that of Hwanung, while another that worshipped the tiger left the area.

Integration between two groups cannot have been easy. Perhaps eating garlic and mugwort and being deprived of sunlight symbolize this difficulty. Some scholars also interpret the 100-day challenge as a kind of coming-of-age ceremony.

Dangun Wanggeom ruled the state founded by the integration of a group that worshipped the bear and the group led by Hwanung. In the story, therefore, he is

Chamseongdan Altar,
Mt. Manisan
One old story tells how
Dangun Wanggeom
once performed rites to
Heaven at this altar on the
summit of Mt. Manisan
on Ganghwado Island. A
rite is still performed here
every year on National
Foundation Day, while
the torch for the National
Athletics Meet is also
lit here. The mountain
is sometimes known as
'Marisan' or 'Meorisan'.

represented as the son of the bear-woman and Hwanung.

So how did Dangun Wanggeom rule the new state? A "*dangun*" was somebody who presided over rituals: a *mudang* (spirit medium), in other words. And a *wanggeom* is somebody with political authority. The term "Dangun Wanggeom," therefore, denotes a supreme ruler in charge of both rituals and politics.

According to the thirteenth-century text *Samguk yusa*, Dangun Wanggeom lived to the age of 1908, then became a mountain god. A person cannot really live for that long, of course, so what does this signify? Perhaps we can interpret it as meaning that several Dangun Wanggeoms ruled in succession.

Both the importance attached to agriculture and the existence of supreme ritual and political rulers are characteristics of the Bronze Age, which tells us when the story of Dangun Wanggeom is set.

Korea, a land of dolmens

Around 40% of all dolmens in the world are located on the Korean Peninsula. There are some 40,000 of them throughout North and South Korea, around half of which - some 20,000 - are in Jeolla-do Province.

Dolmens are the most distinctive form of Bronze Age tomb. Various types exist, ranging from large stones weighing several dozen tonnes to much smaller specimens. Some of them just look like normal rocks at first glance.

The dolmen in the Bugeun-ri area of Ganghwa-do Island has a covering stone that weighs several dozen tonnes alone. Scholars have calculated that it would have taken at least 500 strong men to transport it. Since the typical Bronze Age family consisted of around five people, only one of which would have been a strong man, we can estimate that the individual buried under their dolmen had the power to command at least 2,500

• Various dolmens

Table-form dolmen (above); 'go' board-style dolmen (below); base-type dolmen (below left) Where were bodies buried? With table-form dolmens, the burial chamber was located above the ground; with base-type and *go* board-type dolmens, it was dug into the ground.
Many surviving table-form dolmens have only two supporting stones, but were originally built with four and therefore enclosed on all sides.

people and a lot of hot, sweaty labor. But not all dolmens are the tombs of rulers. Most of them are found in clusters: there's no way that all the tombs in one cluster could belong to such high-ranking figures. Such gatherings of dolmens are generally considered to be joint burial sites of a leader and his family, or of a certain group.

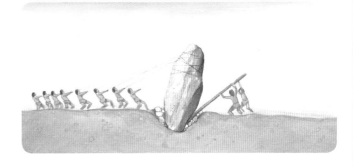

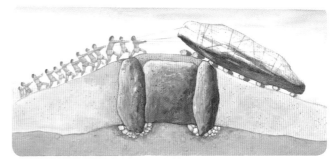

How to build a table-form dolmen
First, erect the supporting stones. Next, pile up earth around them to create a slope up to their tops. Using log rollers and ropes, pull the crowning stone up until it rests on the supporting stones. The earth can then be removed from around the supporting stones. Finally, lay the deceased to rest in the tomb and seal the entrance.

CHAPTER 4

How was
life in Gojoseon?

One piece of Gojoseon earthenware, which dates from around the 4th-5th century BC, features two letters or characters similar to the Chinese character "火" (fire). If these are Gojoseon characters, it would mean that they represent Korea's first indigenous writing system, one invented centuries before Hangeul. Nothing more precise than this is yet known, however. So much about Gojoseon remains shrouded in mystery, even today.

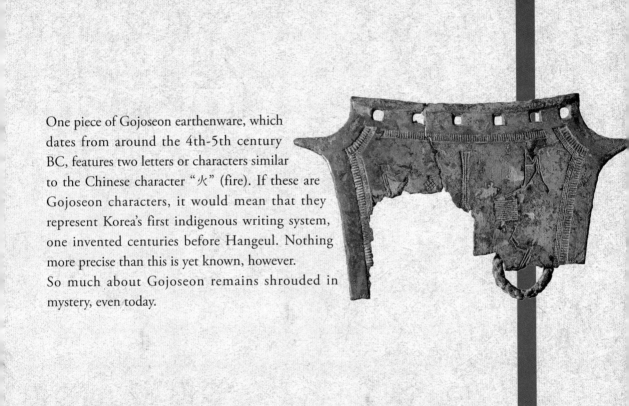

TIME LINE

C. 700000 B.C.

Paleolithic period
Stone tools

C. 8000 B.C.

Neolithic period
Earthenware made from clay; agriculture begins

C. 2300 B.C.

Gojoseon founded
Dangun Wanggeom foundation myth

When did Dangun Wanggeom found Gojoseon? According to Samguk yusa, *it was around 2300 BC. These days, however, scholars place the date much later, at a point after the beginning of the Bronze Age. The exact date remains unknown.*

How far did the territory of Gojoseon extend? And where was Asadal, its capital, located? Different scholars offer various opinions. Some say it was centered in Manchuria and extended west to Bohai Bay and south to the Yeseonggang River. Others believe it was centered in Pyeongyang, in the vicinity of the Daedonggang River. Still others claim it initially had its capital in Manchuria, then relocated to Pyeongyang and the Daedonggang River area.

Gojoseon lasted a considerably long time, from the Bronze Age into the Iron Age. A large number of mysteries surrounding this era are yet to be solved. I suppose it's up to us to do as much research as it takes to find the answers.

Well then, let's take a closer look at some of the mysteries of Gojoseon.

C. 1000 B.C.

Bronze Age
Bronze swords and
mirrors

C. 400 B.C.

Iron Age
Iron weapons and
farming implements

C. 37 B.C.

Goguryeo founded
Jumong establishes
Goguryeo at Jolbon

427

Goguryeo
Capital moved to
Pyeongyang

The people of Gojoseon lived together in villages. In this respect, they were the same as their Neolithic forebears. People in each village worked collectively to farm their crops, using tools made of stone. As I mentioned earlier, bronze was highly valuable and difficult to make. It was only much later, when people began using iron, that metal farming tools were produced.

Clothing, food and housing in Gojoseon

Rice farming began around the 10th century BC. In addition to rice, the people of Gojoseon grew crops such as soy

Bronze with agricultural design
This bronze is engraved with images of people farming. On the right is a man tilling a field with a "*ttabi*," a tool used for deeply ploughing the soil. The development of tools like this in the Bronze Age allowed the production of greater amounts of grain.
– National Museum of Korea

Bronze Age village
This site in Geomdan-ri, Ulsan, was once home to a Bronze Age village. Its overall shape is oval, with maximum and minimum diameters of 118 and 70 meters, respectively. A moat was dug around the perimeter to keep out uninvited guests. The site was covered with earth again following its excavation, so that all you can see there now is a flat piece of land.

History of the chilli
Chillies reached Korea during the Joseon period, following the Imjin Wars. In other words, there was no red, spicy food made with chilli powder before this time.

beans, several types of millet, and sorghum. They also further developed animal husbandry techniques, keeping dogs, pigs, cows, horses and other animals.

Cookery techniques, too, grew more advanced with the introduction of seasonings such as salt, *doenjang* (fermented soy bean paste) and soy sauce. The garlic and mugwort that appear in the Dangun Wanggeom story were commonly used as seasonings and in side dishes. By the way, the garlic used at this time was not the same as what we eat today. It was more similar to what we now know as wild chives. The garlic you and I eat came to Korea in the Iron Age.

The people of Gojoseon also had kimchi. It was different, of course, from today's versions and consisted of radish pickled in salt. It was neither red not hot, since there were no chillies in Korea at the time.

Food consisted of staple grains with wild edible greens like ferns, bellflower, water parsley and *deodeok* (a mountain herb with tasty, nutritious roots), and accompanied by fish such as trout, salmon, mackerel, pollack and atka mackerel, and other side dishes including oysters, conches, freshwater snails, abalone and mussels.

Rice was grown, but was a precious commodity. Like meat, it was only eaten at feasts or rituals. And there was alcohol, of course, brewed from grain or fruit.

Dishes used at this time were made of earth or wood. Since earthenware doesn't decompose, there are still some specimens left in museums today, but everything made of wood back then has rotted away by now.

Food was served in earthenware or wooden dishes and eaten with spoons made from animal bones or wood. Take a look at earthenware from this time, though, and you'll see how much more varied it is than that of previous periods, and that, most notably, the comb patterns have disappeared. It's a dull brown color, with no pattern. This is known as plain earthenware. Fired in kilns, it's less pretty than comb-pattern pottery but much stronger.

Clothes were made from hemp, wool and silk. Most people wore straw shoes, but those of high social status wore leather footwear and hats. The skins of leopards and tigers caught in Gojoseon were of high enough quality to be exported to China.

Housebuilding, too, was much more highly developed than that of the Neolithic period. Houses were generally half-dugouts, built slightly closer to ground level than their Neolithic predecessors. As before, the ground

Semilunar stone knives
Stone knives such as these were widely used in the Bronze Age to cut ears of ripened grain. Cords were threaded through the holes in order to attach the knife to the user's wrist. Though most knives were half-moon-shaped, some were triangular or square.
−National Museum of Korea

Plain earthenware
These kiln-fired plain earthenware vessels have smooth sides and flat bases. They are much harder than comb-pattern earthenware.
−National Museum of Korea

'Jjokgudeul'

Ondol is a brilliant heating system. In Gojoseon, however, there was no full-floor heating. Instead, heating stones known as *jjokgudeul* were placed in one part of the room only. The *jjokgudeul* in this photo were discovered in the village of Sejuk-ri in Yeongbyeon, Pyeonganbuk-do Province.

was dug, thick wooden poles were erected, and rafters placed on top of them and covered with straw. The forms of dwellings, though, were now much more sophisticated and included conical and square designs. Straw left over from thatching the roof was woven into mats that were laid on the floor, stopping the damp that rose from below.

Homes were heated by large stones known as *jjokgudeul* on one side. No longer built underground like Neolithic dwellings, they would have been unbearably cold without additional heating systems. That's why somebody invented *jjokgudeul*. Once heated to a high temperature, these large rocks would stay hot through the night, keeping the house warm.

Large households built big homes, divided into several rooms: society had now moved beyond single-room dwellings. Storehouses were built next to homes for keeping the grain harvested by each household.

The Song of Yeook

Koreans' love of singing and dancing is a deep-rooted national characteristic. The people of Gojoseon loved both of these, too. Whenever they held a harvest festival in honor of heaven, much singing and dancing would take place.

If you're wondering what kind of songs and dances these were, there's one clue that can point us in the right direction: a song called *Gongmu doha ga*, included in the ancient Chinese text *Gujinzhu* ("Notes to Things Old and New"). Unfortunately, this version of the song only describes the lyrics of the song and we have no way of knowing its melody or rhythm.

Gongmu doha ga was written by Yeook, the wife of a boatman called Gwangnijago. It comes with an amazing background story.

One day, Gwangnijago was sitting on the riverbank when a white-haired old man ran up to the river and jumped into the water. His wife ran after him, begging him to stop, but he ended up sinking below the surface and drowning. The wife sang a sad song while playing on a *gonghu* (a harp-like instrument), then threw herself into the water after her husband.

Gwangnijago went home and told his wife, Yeook, what he had seen. Yeook then took up her own *gonghu* and improvised a song on the spot.

'Gonghu'
This string instrument, popular in Gojoseon, is similar to a Western-style harp. It comes in various forms, with names such as *wagonghu*, *sugonghu*, *daegonghu* and *sogonghu*. Originally a Central Asian instrument, the *gonghu* made its way to Korea via China.

'Gongmu doha ga'
This song by a Gojoseon woman has survived all the way to the present.

My love, don't cross the water!

But still, you cross

Dying in the river.

Oh, my love, what am I to do?

Gojoseon stemmed dish
inscribed with characters

The fact that Yeook was able to compose and sing a song like this in impromptu fashion suggests that the people of Gojoseon loved music and were talented composers.

Did Gojoseon have a writing system? Its rulers learned and used Chinese characters, while most common people were illiterate. There is one piece of Gojoseon earthenware, which dates from around the 4th-5th century BC, that features two letters or characters similar to the Chinese character "火" (fire). If these are Gojoseon characters, it would mean that they represent Korea's first indigenous writing system, one invented centuries before Hangeul. Nothing more precise than this is yet known, however.

So much about Gojoseon remains shrouded in mystery, even today.

The development of Wiman Joseon

From 206 BC, when the state founded by Emperor Qin Shi Huang fell, war raged uninterrupted in China for almost

The extent of Gojoseon territory

- Gojoseon territory
- Table-form dolmen site
- Bronze dagger discovery site

Mt. Baekdusan

Gojosen

Mt. Myohyangsan

EAST SEA

Mt. Manisan

YELLOW SEA

five years until the establishment of the Han Dynasty. During this time, a large number of Chinese war refugees arrived in Gojoseon. Among them was a figure named Wiman.

Wiman brought around 1,000 followers with him from Yan in China. His hair was done up in a topknot and he was wearing Gojoseon-style clothes when he arrived, which leads some to believe he was not Chinese but a Gojoseon Korean who had been living in Yan.

At this time, Gojoseon was ruled by King Jun. The king placed deep trust in Wiman, making him a government official of the high *baksa* rank and putting him in charge of a swathe territory 100 *ri* wide in the western part of the state. In 194 BC, however, after secretly building up his own power base, Wiman overthrew the King and took the throne for himself. Jun sailed away to the state of Jin, in the southern part of the Korean Peninsula.

Under Wiman's leadership, Gojoseon grew more powerful by the day. The Iron Age was already beginning, allowing the production of more grain using metal farm implements and the creation of powerful military forces armed with iron weapons. Gojoseon's power structure solidified, with government positions such as minister, magistrate and general created beneath the king.

The state became even more powerful under Wiman's grandson, King Ugeo. It secured a monopoly on trade with the Han dynasty in China by preventing Jin, to the south, and other states from engaging in direct exchange with Han. Gojoseon was now one of the major powers of Northeast Asia.

Feeling threatened by the growth of his Korean neighbor, Han Emperor Wu sent an envoy named Shehe to demand that Gojoseon serve Han. Gojoseon, however, refused to be bowed.

On his way home, the Chinese envoy killed Biwang Jang of Gojoseon. He reported back to Emperor Wu: "I've killed the commander of Joseon." The emperor then appointed to the position of commander of "Liaodong Dongbu Duwei" (East Liaodong Commandery).

Angered by this turn of events, King Ugeo killed the Han commander in a daring ambush. When Emperor Wu learned of this, he was secretly pleased. He now took Shehe's death as an excuse to plan an invasion of Gojoseon.

Emperor Wu mobilized his army and navy and attacked from two directions. 7,000 troops under Admiral Yangfu

Crossbow
The crossbow was a powerful new weapon. Releasing its arrow at the pull of a trigger, it delivered a shot far more accurate and destructive than that of a hand-drawn bow. The photo below shows the trigger mechanism of a crossbow.

sailed across the Yellow Sea, while 50,000 under the command of General-of-the-Left Xunzhi invaded overland, via Liaodong. Xunzhi confidently believed he would take a city like Wanggeomseong, the Gojoseon capital, in no time. But the brave warriors of Gojoseon won an outright victory in the first battle of the war.

Wanggeomseong: Gojoseon's last stand

Besieged by the Han army, the people of Wanggeomseong shut their city gates and fought. As time went by, the Chinese

 Gojoseon Law: the 'Eight Transgressions'

The Chinese history book *Hanshu* ("Book of Han") records that Gojoseon had a system called the "Eight Transgressions." These were the country's laws - here are three of them: "Anyone who kills another will be put to death. Anyone who injures another must pay compensation in grain. Anyone who steals will become the slave of the household from which he or she stole. Those wishing to avoid a sentence of slavery must pay 500,000 in 'money'."

The Eight Transgressions allow us to guess at the social order of Gojoseon. This was a society that acknowledged and protected private property, including slave ownership. Slaves worked for their owners; if an owner died, his slaves were obliged to die too. This practice was known as *sunjang* and involved burying slaves alive with their deceased owners. At the time, people believed that dying meant passing on to another world. They took their slaves from this life with them in order to ensure a comfortable existence in the next.

The Battle of Wanggeomseong
The people of Gojoseon fought bravely for about a year from within the earthen fortress of Wanggeomseong. Eventually, however, their state fell in the summer of 108 B.C.

forces began to lose morale. Within the capital, too, opinion became divided between those who wanted to keep on fighting and those who wanted to make peace.

The main advocate of peacemaking was minister Yeokgyegyeong. When King Ugeo ignored his opinion, he left the capital and headed south. Officials such as minister Noin, Haneum, Cham and General Wanggyeop also called for peace. Eventually, they killed Ugeo and surrendered to Han. Despite the king's death, Wanggeomseong did not collapse. Its people now carried on fighting under the leadership of an official named Seonggi. Xunzhi decided to look for other ways of winning the war, in the belief that Wanggeomseong could not be taken by force. He had Seonggi killed by King Ugeo's son, Jang, and Noin's son, Choe. Finally, with Seonggi dead, Wanggeomseong fell. After a year of bloody war, Gojoseon

Nangnang Fortress
This low earthen fortress near the Daedonggang River in Pyeongyang is said to have been built by the people of Han where Wanggeomseong, the Gojoseon capital, once stood.

was no more. It was 108 BC.

The people of Gojoseon were taken off to faraway China. Those who had betrayed the fallen state were rewarded with government positions in Han dynasty. Ultimately, Gojoseon was destroyed by division and treachery in its ruling class, not as a result of military defeat.

Han now built four commanderies to rule over what had been Gojoseon territory: Nangnang (Lelang), Imdun (Lintun), Hyeondo (Xuantu) and Jinbeon (Zhenfan). Faced with strong resistance from the former citizens of Gojoseon, however, Zhenfan and Lintun commanderies soon disappeared and Xuantu Commandery was driven west. Nangnang Commandery remained, before eventually falling to Goguryeo in 313.

Well then, that's probably enough for today. We've seen how Gojoseon, the first state in Korean history, flourished and fell over the course of several centuries. There's no need to memorize all of the many incidents that took place during this long period. History is not about remembering facts; it's about feeling and thinking. Just developing a sense of its pulse is enough.

Gojoseon: originally just 'Joseon'

Gojoseon was at first simply called Joseon. The first use of the name Gojoseon appears in *Samguk yusa*. Iryeon added the Chinese character "古" ("old") in order to distinguish Gojoseon from a later state with the same name. So what is the "later" Joseon that Iryeon had in mind?

Surely it must be the Joseon dynasty founded in 1392 by Yi Seonggye?

No - think a bit harder. Iryeon wrote *Samguk yusa* in the Goryeo dynasty, well before Yi Seonggye founded his Joseon. To foresee the arrival of this new state in advance would have been an impressive feat of prophecy by anyone's standards. In fact, Iryeon used the term Gojoseon to distinguish this state from that ruled by Wiman.

Did books predating *Samguk yusa* also mention Dangun Wanggeom? Almost certainly. Unfortunately, however, none of them remain today. Nonetheless, *Samguk sagi* ("History of the Three Kingdoms"), compiled by historian Kim Busik around 100 years earlier than *Samguk yusa*, contains no trace of Dangun Wanggeom. Why? Because Kim Busik, a Confucian scholar, regarded the story as superstitious nonsense.

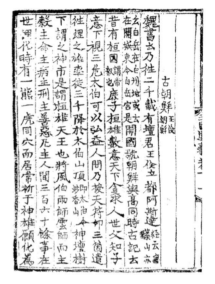

The passage on Gojoseon in 'Samguk yusa'

CHAPTER 5

What came after Gojoseon?

Gojoseon, Buyeo, Goguryeo, Dongye and Okjeo were all located in northern areas of the Korean Peninsula. What, then, was going on further south? Surely the southern regions of the peninsula can't have been completely uninhabited, what with everything that was going on further north?

There were, of course, people here too. Humans settled in any part of the Korean Peninsula where they found good living environments, gathering in villages and founding their own states. Among these, the stronger states often conquered their neighbors and became even larger.

TIME LINE

C. 700000 B.C.	C. 8000 B.C.	C. 2300 B.C.
Paleolithic period Stone tools	**Neolithic period** Earthenware made from clay; agriculture begins	**Gojoseon founded** Dangun Wanggeom foundation myth

You may have experienced some confusion over the name "Buyeo" - was it a town or a state? The answer, in fact, is both.
And they were in completely different places.
The town of Buyeo is located in today's Chungcheongnam-do Province and was once the capital of Baekje during the Three Kingdoms period.
The state known as Buyeo, however, was in Manchuria.
If you look at a map, you'll see a long river that meanders down from Mt. Baekdusan into Manchuria. This is the Songhuajiang River, and it's surrounded by a large plain. It was here that the state of Buyeo was once located.
Today, then, let's have a look at Buyeo and the other states that feature in Korean history after the fall of Gojoseon.

C. 1000 B.C.	C. 400 B.C.	C. 37 B.C.	427
Bronze Age	**Iron Age**	**Goguryeo founded**	**Goguryeo**
Bronze swords and mirrors	Iron weapons and farming implements	Jumong establishes Goguryeo at Jolbon	Capital moved to Pyeongyang

The state of Buyeo was founded shortly before the fall of Gojoseon and lasted for around 600 years. Which is to say that it was the second Korean state in history. Several more states also appeared at this time: Goguryeo, Dongye, Okjeo and the Samhan confederacies. There may even have been a few others, too. But since no history book contains an accurate record, we can't know for sure.

Even about these states, we know very little. No records written by their people remain, and only a small amount of archaeological evidence survives. Volume 30 of *Weishu* ("Book of Wei") in the Chinese historical text *Sanguozhi* ("Record of the Three Kingdoms"), however, contains comparatively detailed records of these states. Most of

'Biography of Eastern Barbarians'
Sanguozhi is a historical text that covers the Three Kingdoms period of Chinese history, when figures such as Cao Cao, Liu Fei, Zhuge Liang and Sun Quan were active in the states of Wei, Wu and Shu. It was written at the end of the third century AD by Chen Shou of the Jin Dynasty. The part of the text that covers the history of Wei is known as *Weishu* and contains *Dongyizhuan* - literally meaning "biography of eastern barbarians." The Chinese believed that their country was the center of the world, and that other lands were inhabited by barbarians. *Dongyizhuan* contains records of the states of Buyeo, Goguryeo, Okjeo, Dongye and the Samhan confederacies. Though these records are written from a Chinese perspective, we have no choice but to refer to them given the lack of other sources.

what I'm going to tell you today comes from this book.

Traces of Buyeo

Buyeo was founded around the third century BC. It has its own foundation myth, according to which its founder was a figure called Dongmyeong. He was born from an egg laid by a lady-in-waiting on intimate terms with the King of Tuoli, a state to the north of Buyeo. Dongmyeong was an outstanding archer. He founded Buyeo after fleeing south to escape his jealous enemies.

Have you heard the story of Jumong, the founder of Goguyreo? It's almost exactly the same as that of Dongmyeong: both figures hatched from eggs, both were excellent archers and both fled south and founded new

Tomb of King Dongmyeong
This is the tomb of Jumong, founder of Goguryeo. Located in Pyeongyang, in today's North Korea, it is believed to have been built some time in the late-4th or early-5th century, around the time Goguryeo moved its capital to Pyeongyang. The tomb was probably relocated here from elsewhere.

states. Not only that: the people of Goguryeo even believed that Dongmyeong and Jumong were the same person. Why?

I'll mention this again later on, but Goguryeo was founded by people who had left Buyeo. Goguryeo then became more powerful than Buyeo itself and, before long, made a slight tweak to the Buyeo foundation myth by replacing Dongmyeong with Jumong. So now you know why the two stories are so similar.

By the way, there are also plenty of similarities between Baekje and Buyeo. In fact, Buyeo was the surname of the kings of Baekje. And during the reign of King Seong of Baekje, the capital was relocated to Sabi (now named Buyeo, in Chungcheongnam-do Province) and the country's name changed to Nambuyeo ("South Buyeo").

This happened because Baekje believed its roots lay in Buyeo. As an offshoot of Goguryeo, Baekje became a powerful competitor of the latter. Rather than be regarded as a spin-off of its arch-rival, it wanted to emphasize its ancestral connections to Buyeo.

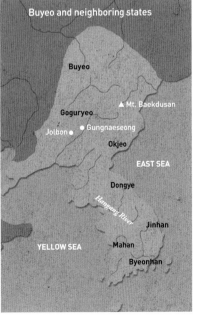

The livestock farmers of Buyeo

Around the time that Gojoseon fell, Buyeo was the most powerful state in the Manchurian region. Its people had earned a reputation for their livestock raising culture, in particular. They raised horses, pigs, cows, chickens and dogs, but were most famous for their horses. The horses of Buyeo were tall and fast, and known as *myeongma* ("excellent horses") or *sinma* ("beautiful horses").

Even the titles of high-ranking Buyeo officials offer us an idea of the high esteem in which they held their animals. The top four officials were the four "*ga:*" *maga, uga, jeoga* and *guga*. *Ma* (馬), *u* (牛), *jeo* (猪) and *gu* (狗) meant horse, cow, pig and dog, respectively, while *ga* was a respectful term for an esteemed or great person. Pretty funny names in today's context.

Each of the four *ga* was responsible for ruling over one region. The king only ruled directly over the central part of the state, while the rest of its territory was divided into four regions ruled by the *ga* and known collectively as the *sachuldo*. The central region contained facilities like palaces, storehouses and prisons.

It appears that, in their respective regions, the four *ga* were effectively like kings. Which means that the power of the actual king would not have been all that great. If he made the wrong political move, the four *ga* might force him off the throne. When life became hard for the people, in times of flood or drought, the king would be held responsible and overthrown, if not killed.

Did Buyeo have laws, like Gojoseon? We only know about

four of its legal articles today: going by these, Buyeo law was stricter than that of Gojoseon.

One Buyeo code, known as the "*Ilchaek sibi beop*" ("Twelvefold Law") stipulates that anyone found guilty of theft must repay the victim twelve times the value of what was stolen. The families of murderers were taken as slaves, too, which suggests that Buyeo, like Gojoseon, had a system of slavery. The fact that excessively jealous wives were put to death, meanwhile, indicates that Buyeo was a very male-centered society.

When it comes to the appearance of Buyeo people, all we can do is take the limited historical resources we have and use our imagination to fill in the gaps. They were big, courageous people, who twisted their hair into buns like the topknots worn by people in the Joseon period. Their clothes were made of white hemp fabric and their jackets had very wide sleeves.

What's interesting is that the people of Buyeo loved singing, and sang even as they walked around. They must have led very happy lives, their streets full of song all day long.

That's enough about Buyeo - now let's look at Okjeo and Dongye.

Buyeo law
- Murderers shall be put to death and their families taken as slaves.
- Thieves must repay their victims twelve times the value of what they steal.
- Adulterers shall be put to death.
- Excessively jealous wives shall be put to death.

Buyeo golden belt buckles These buckles depict horses in relief. Could these be the beautiful horses of which Buyeo was so proud? Its people were also outstanding goldsmiths.

Okjeo and Dongye: similar to Goguryeo

Okjeo was located near the coast of what are today North and South Hamgyeong provinces in North Korea. This was an area rich in seafood and home to salt production. Salt was regarded as a highly valuable commodity as people then, just as today, could not live without it.

The people of Okjeo were similar to those of Goguryeo in several regards including their food, clothing, etiquette and brave, upright characters. Their marriage customs, at least, were different. When a Goguryeo couple got married, the groom would go to live in the bride's household. In Okjeo, the opposite happened: when a woman reached 10 years of age, she would go to live in the household of her future husband until she became an adult, at which time the groom would make a payment to her family and marry her. The practice of raising a girl in the house of her future in-laws is known in Korean as the *minmyeoneuri* system. Isn't it strange that Goguryeo and Okjeo, such similar countries, had diametrically opposed marriage customs? Even scholars have yet to make sense of this.

Dongye, meaning "Eastern Ye," was located in the northern part of today's Gangwon-do Province. Like Okjeo, its language and customs were similar to those of Goguryeo. It seems probable that the ancestors of the people

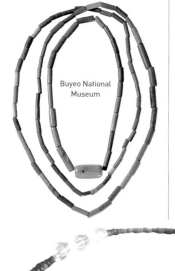

Jade necklaces
Rulers liked to adorn themselves in accessories made of gemstones. The jade necklaces in these photos were excavated at Dongseo-ri in Yesan, Chungcheongnam-do (above) and at Nopo-dong in Busan (below).

Buyeo National Museum

Busan Museum

of Okjeo and Dongye came from Buyeo or Goguryeo.

The bows and horses of Dongye were renowned even in China. Known as *dangung* (檀弓), Dongye bows were small but powerful and had a long range. Dongye horses, meanwhile, were known as *gwahama* ("horses [small enough] to pass [even under the low branches of] fruit trees"). They were small but tough and mild in temperament, making them easy to handle.

Okjeo and Dongye failed to grow into strong states like Goguryeo. They fell under the control of the latter, which ended up incorporating them completely. In this, they were not alone: Buyeo, too, was conquered by and became part of Goguryeo.

After starting out as a small state, Goguryeo grew bigger as it kept conquering smaller states around it such as Okjeo, Dongye and Buyeo. We'll take a closer look at Goguryeo later on.

Samhan: A collection of some eighty states

Until now, we've been concentrating on Manchuria and the northern regions of the Korean Peninsula. Gojoseon, Buyeo, Goguryeo, Dongye and Okjeo were all located in this area. What, then, was going on further south? Surely the southern regions of

Locations of the Samhan
EAST SEA
Baekjeguk
Hangang River
Mokjiguk
Mahan
Jinhan
YELLOW SEA
Saroguk
Byeonhan

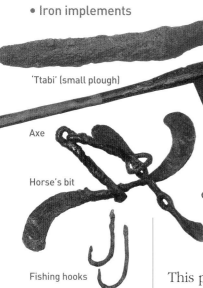

• Iron implements

'Ttabi' (small plough)

Axe

Horse's bit

Fishing hooks

These items were discovered at Daho-ri in Changwon, Gyeongsangnam-do Province. Iron farming tools allowed the production of greater quantities of food than before.
–National Museum of Korea

the peninsula can't have been completely uninhabited, what with everything that was going on further north?

There were, of course, people here too. Humans settled in any part of the Korean Peninsula where they found good living environments, gathering in villages and founding their own states. Among these, the stronger states often conquered their neighbors and became even larger. This process happened in various places.

With its warm climate, wide plains and large rivers, the southern part of the Korean Peninsula has made a good place for humans to live since long ago and seen the emergence of many states. Around eighty small states existed in this area, joined in entities named Mahan, Jinhan and Byeonhan. Collectively, these three confederacies are known as the Samhan ("Three Han").

Mahan consisted of fifty-four small states located in today's Jeolla-do, Chungcheong-do and Gyeonggi-do provinces. Jinhan comprised twelve small states in the vicinity of today's Daegu and Gyeongju, while Byeonhan was also a collection of twelve small states, situated in today's Gimhae, near Masan. What we know today as the kingdom of Silla had its roots in Saro, one of the small states in the Jinhan confederation, while Baekje began as a small state in Mahan.

Agriculture was the most important means of living for the people of the Samhan. They grew a lot of rice, in the cultivation of which water is of paramount importance. The people of the Samhan therefore built reservoirs to store rainwater for irrigation. Some of the reservoirs built at this time, such as Uirimji in Jecheon, Byeokgolje in Gimje and Susanje in Miryang, still exist.

The states I've mentioned today - Buyeo, Goguryeo, Dongye, Okjeo and the Samhan - were found in various parts of Manchuria and the Korean Peninsula before the Three Kingdoms period, from the Bronze Age to the Iron Age. It's easy not to pay much attention to this part of Korean history, but I think it's actually very important. If you knew nothing about it, you might assume the Three Kingdoms had suddenly emerged from some kind of long vacuum after the fall of Gojoseon. In fact, they slowly evolved from some of the smaller states that existed at this time.

Uirimji Reservoir, Jecheon
The people of the Samhan built reservoirs in order to store rainwater for future use. The reservoir in this photo is Uirimji in Jecheon, Chungcheongbuk-do Province. One story tells that it was built by U Reuk during the reign of King Jinheung of Silla, but it is believed to date from much earlier, in the Samhan period.

What was the purpose of 'jecheon haengsa?'

Every December according to the lunar calendar, all the people of Buyeo gathered and held a rite in honor of the heavens. Such ceremonies, also held in Goguryeo, Dongye and the Samhan, were known as *"jecheon haengsa"* ("rites to Heaven"). They were very important to people at this time, reflecting in turn the importance of agriculture. If a good harvest was to be enjoyed, the right temperature was needed and rain and sunlight had to come down from heaven at the right time. This is why people worshipped the sky as a god who could deliver abundant harvests and preserve life, and why *jecheon haengsa* were a spiritual anchor and a religion.

The trials of criminals also took place at these events. Enumerating the crimes of the accused and punishing her or him in front of everybody must have served as quite a powerful deterrent to others.

Each state had a slightly different name for its *jecheon haengsa* and held it at a slightly different time. That of Buyeo was called the Yeonggo (迎鼓), which meant "greeting god while banging on the drum." Dongye held its main festival every year in October according to the lunar calendar and called it the Mucheon (舞天), meaning "dancing for the heavens." In the Samhan, festivals were held in May, after seeds were sown, and in October after the

Sotdae at Seokje Village, Buan, Jeollabuk-do
This stone duck provides protection for the village.

harvest. Rites in the Samhan were held in places known as "*sodo*." To show that *sodo* were sacred, the people of Samhan erected huge tree trunks there, from which they hung bells and drums. Doesn't that sound similar to the tall, symbolic *sotdae* poles we still sometimes put up today? Even fugitive criminals could not be caught if they took refuge in a *sodo*. These rites were also opportunities to develop spiritual bonds, just like some of the rallies and retreats that Koreans use to encourage solidity today. And they were a form of festival. After the ceremony itself, all people - male, female, young and old - came together as one and spent the night singing and dancing. It must have been quite a sight.

'Sotdae' at Gangmun Village, Gangwon-do Province
Birds were once regarded as messengers that connected people with the sky. The villagers probably put up *sotdae* with birds atop them in order to convey their wishes to Heaven.

Fern-pattern ironwork (left)
and ritual vessel with three dried persimmon (right)
These Samhan artifacts were unearthed at Daho-ri in Changwon, Gyeongsangnam-do Province
– National Museum of Korea

CHAPTER 6

The founding of the Three Kingdoms and Gaya

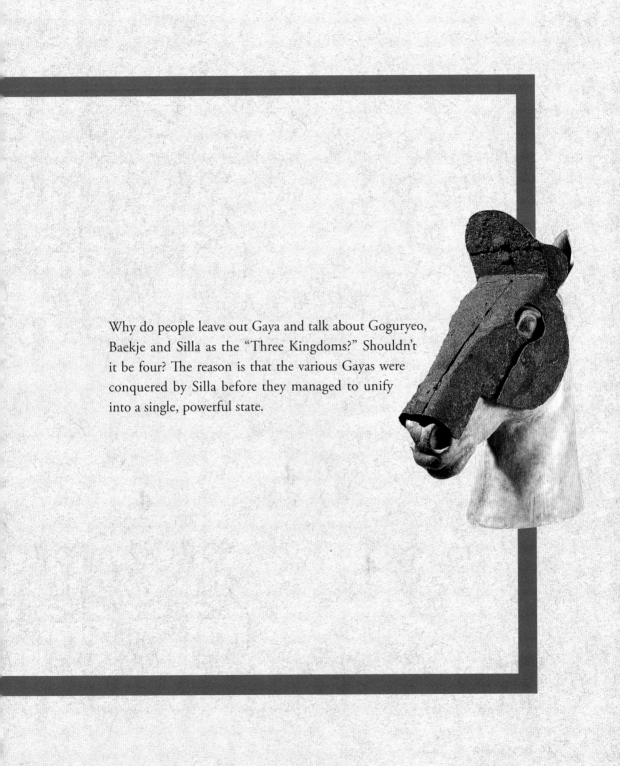

Why do people leave out Gaya and talk about Goguryeo, Baekje and Silla as the "Three Kingdoms?" Shouldn't it be four? The reason is that the various Gayas were conquered by Silla before they managed to unify into a single, powerful state.

| TIME LINE | | | C. 700000 B.C. | | | C. 8000 B.C. | | | C. 2300 B.C. | |

Paleolithic period
Stone tools

Neolithic period
Earthenware made from clay; agriculture begins

Gojoseon founded
Dangun Wanggeom foundation myth

In my last letter, I wrote about the states that came after Gojoseon. Today, we'll see how three states among them - Goguryeo, Baekje and Silla - vanquished all the others and came out on top.

Just like Gojoseon, Goguryeo, Baekje and Silla all had their own mystical stories about distant founding ancestors - stories that have outlived these old states to reach us even today. As I said before, such myths are not unique to Korea but found among peoples all over the world. They say Romulus and Remus, the twin brothers who founded Rome, were suckled and brought up by a she-wolf, while Yu the Great, the founder of China's Xia Dynasty, is said to have been born from the corpse of his father, which had not decomposed. And legend has it that King Gilgamesh of Uruk was half god, half man.

With their strange and mystical content, foundation myths inspire a sense of awe and respect for ancestors. So, what are the foundation myths of Goguryeo, Baekje and Silla, and what do they actually mean?

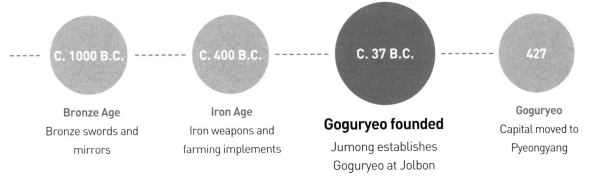

C. 1000 B.C.

C. 400 B.C.

C. 37 B.C.

427

Bronze Age
Bronze swords and mirrors

Iron Age
Iron weapons and farming implements

Goguryeo founded
Jumong establishes Goguryeo at Jolbon

Goguryeo
Capital moved to Pyeongyang

One day, sometime after the fall of Gojoseon, King Geumwa of Dongbuyeo was walking along the banks of a river called Ubalsu, to the south of Mt. Taebaeksan, when he met a woman.

"My name is Yuhwa and I am the daughter of Habaek, the god of the river," she said. "While I was playing with my sisters, a man appeared and said he was Hae Mosu, the son of Heaven. He took me to his home on the banks of the Amnokgang River, below Mt. Ungsimsan, married me and then left. My parents scolded me for getting married without their permission and banished me to this place."

King Geumwa took Yuhwa to his palace. A while later, she laid an enormous egg.

Hunting scene from a mural in Muyongchong Tomb
This Goguryeo tomb mural depicts hunters drawing bows with all their strength on the backs of galloping horses. What do you think - does it give you a sense of the might of the people of Goguryeo?

Would you believe it: a human laying an egg? Thinking it inauspicious, Geumwa ordered that the egg be taken from the palace and cast out into the wilderness. But the wild beasts didn't even touch it. Geumwa tried to break it, but the egg, strangely, would not crack. Unable to think of anything else, he gave it back to Yuhwa.

Jumong: master archer and founder of Goguryeo

Yuhwa wrapped the egg in cloth and left it in a warm place. Presently, it hatched and a baby came out. It was a radiant young boy. When he was only seven years old, the boy made himself a bow and arrows. He never missed a shot. They named him Jumong, which meant "brilliant archer" in the language of Buyeo.

Geumwa had seven sons of his own, all of whom were jealous of Jumong and his many talents. One day, Yuhwa learned that the seven sons were plotting to kill Jumong. She told her son to run away. Of course, he already knew what Geumwa's sons were planning.

Jumong fled south with three men, Oi, Mari and Hyeopbo. On their way, they came to a river called Eomsisu. Their pursuers were rapidly approaching, but they couldn't cross the water as they had no boat. Jumong called out in despair:

"I am the grandson of the Emperor of Heaven and Habaek.

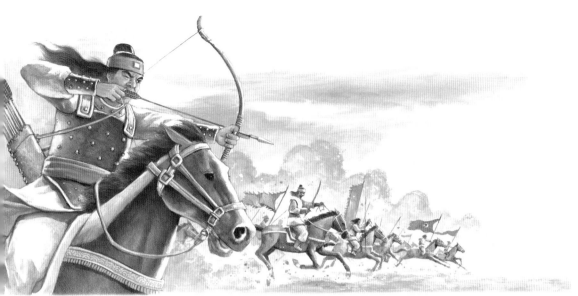

My pursuers are about to catch me - what shall I do?"

Straight away, a multitude of fish and turtles appeared and formed a bridge in the water with their bodies. After crossing safely, Jumong arrived in a place called Jolbon. There, he founded his own state and became king. He named his new country Goguryeo. He was twenty-two years old.

This is the foundation myth of Goguryeo. It appears in both *Samguk sagi* ("History of the Three Kingdoms") and *Samguk yusa*. According to the story, Jumong's father was King Hae Mosu of Bukbuyeo ("North Buyeo") and son of the Emperor of Heaven - of celestial descent, in other words. And his mother, Yuhwa, was the daughter of Habaek, who probably ruled the Ubalsu region.

So Jumong was born to Hae Mosu, king of Bukbuyeo, and the daughter of Habaek, lived in Dongbuyeo, the country of

Jumong, founder of Goguryeo
Jumong was an excellent archer. In fact, that's precisely what his name meant in the language of Buyeo. On the Gwanggaeto Stele, though, he is mentioned not as Jumong but as "Chumo." This is because various different Chinese characters have been used to represent the pronunciation of his name. The story of Jumong is told slightly differently in *Samguk sagi* and *Samguk yusa*. The former claims that Jumong was twenty-two years old when he founded his country, while the latter puts this age at twelve. And *Samguk sagi* mentions Mt. Ungsimsan and a river called Eomsisu, whereas *Samguk yusa* records them as Mt. Ungsinsan and Eomsu. In this book, I've followed *Samguk sagi*.

WunüShancheng Mountain Fortress
This fortress is located in Huanren Manchu Autonomous County in today's Liaoning Province, China. It is thought to have been the site of the first Goguryeo capital. With sheer cliffs on three sides and deep valley on the fourth, it would have made an ideal stronghold, almost impossible to attack. The wide, flat area on top of the mountain, with space to build around 300 spacious houses, and a spring that never runs dry, made it suitable for human habitation.

Former site of Gungnaeseong Fortress
These are the ruins of Gungnaeseong Fortress, located in what is now the city of Ji'an in Jilin Province, Manchuria. Gungnaeseong became the capital of Goguryeo during the reign of King Yuri, a status that it maintained for around 420 years until the capital was relocated once again, to Pyeongyang. These days the fortress has largely been destroyed and is surrounded by apartment blocks, making it hard to imagine its original appearance.

King Geumwa, and later fled south and founded Goguryeo.

Jolbon, where Jumong founded his new state, lay near the Donggagang River, a branch of the Amnokgang River. This corresponds to Huanren in today's Liaoning Province, in China. Jolbon was a mountainous area, ideal as a military stronghold but lacking in good agricultural land to the extent where its people always went hungry, no matter how much effort they put into farming. From its earliest days, then, Goguryeo devoted much energy to fighting and conquering neighboring states in order to acquire flatter land.

Jumong's successor, King Yuri, moved his capital to Gungnaeseong Fortress on the banks of the Amnokgang. From then on, Goguryeo developed as a society, introducing various systems while it fought with its neighbors. It conquered adjacent Buyeo, Okjeo and Dongye and became a powerful state whose land encompassed parts of the Amnokgang basin, Manchuria and northern parts of the Korean Peninsula.

Baekje: the state the people followed gladly

Immediately after the founding of Goguryeo in Jolbon, another new state emerged further south near the Hangang River: Baekje. Its founder was Onjo, son of Jumong.

When Jumong fled Dongbuyeo, he left his pregnant wife behind. In his hurry to escape, he had been unable to take her with him. As he bade his wife farewell, Jumong told her that if she bore a son she must tell him to go and find his father, if and when he survived to majority.

After becoming king in Jolbon, Jumong married a local woman by the name of Soseono, who bore him two sons, Biryu and Onjo. Meanwhile, Yuri, the son born in Dongbuyeo to the wife Jumong had left behind, came to find his father. Jumong took Yuri as his crown prince. When this happened, Biryu and Onjo took Ogan, Maryeo and eight other retainers and a following of commoners and left for lands further south. After a difficult journey, they finally reached Wiryeseong (today's Seoul) and climbed to the top of a mountain called Buaak to survey the surrounding land. After looking around, their retainers spoke:

"This place is ideal for founding a new state. You should choose it as your capital."

But Biryu, the elder brother, wanted to build the capital in nearby Michuhol, the place we now know as the city of

Sungnyeoljeon,
Namhansanseong
Mountain Fortress
This shrine was built in
honor of Onjo, the founder
of Baekje, in the Joseon
period.

**So Seono and the founding
of Baekje**
Samguk sagi contains
another story about the
founding of Baekje. The
story tells of how So Seono
took her two sons, Biryu
and Onjo, and got married to
Jumong following the death
of her husband, Utae. A rich
woman, So Seono was of
great help to Jumong as he
built his new state. When
Jumong made his son, Yuri,
crown prince, however,
Biryu, Onjo and So Seono
headed south together and
founded Baekje. According
to this story, So Seono
contributed greatly to the
founding of both Goguryeo
and Baekje.

Incheon. The retainers tried to talk him out of it, but Biryu left for Michuhol anyway. His younger brother, Onjo, chose Wiryeseong as the site for his capital. He called his new state "Sipje" (十濟) which means either "ten retainers help" or "we crossed ten rivers".

Biryu, who had gone to Michuhol, ended up dying in a state of regret when the salty water turned out to be unsuitable for agriculture and life was hard. The commoners who had followed him there went back to Wiryeseong. Onjo then changed the name of his state to "Baekje" (百濟) meaning "the people followed gladly."

The story of Biryu and Onjo is recorded in *Samguk sagi* and *Samguk yusa*. It tells us that people who broke away from Goguryeo migrated south and founded Baekje near the Hangang River, the site of today's Seoul. Wiryeseong was located in what is now the Gangdong-gu district of Seoul.

Baekje was initially no more than one of the several dozen states that made up Mahan, itself one of the three Samhan confederations. Gradually, however, it expanded its territory through an ongoing series of wars with neighboring states. Onjo began by annexing the Incheon area, which played a vital role in marine transport. This is what is indicated by the part of the foundation myth that tells how "the people of

Baekje stone mound tomb
This style of stone mound tomb is highly similar to that of Goguryeo's Janggunchong Tomb. Some say this makes it clear that Baekje was founded by people who broke away from Goguryeo. The tomb is located in Seokchon-dong, Songpa-gu, Seoul.

Michuhol came to Onjo."

After ten years or so, Baekje had grown into a large state that covered an area extending to the Yeseonggang River in the north, Gongju in the south, Chuncheon in the east and the Yellow Sea in the west. King Geunchogo of Baekje, meanwhile, further expanded its territory down to the south coast of today's Jeolla-do Province and extended its control as far east as the region of the Nakdonggang River.

Baekje thus took control of the central and southern regions of the Korean Peninsula, which became a cause of conflict with Goguryeo.

From Saro to Silla

Once, in the region of today's Gyeongju, there was a small country by the name of Saro. You may remember how I said it was one of the twelve small states that comprised Jinhan.

One day, the head of the village of Yangsanchon in Saro

Site of Najeong Well,
Gyeongju
Najeong is the well by
which Bak Hyeokgeose
hatched from his egg.

saw a white horse kneeling down and crying beside a well called Najeong. When he went to take a closer look, he saw a huge, purple egg. Lo and behold, a young child hatched from it. Doesn't that sound similar to the birth of Jumong? Awed by the birth of the child, the people of Saro waited until he was thirteen years old, then made him their king. They gave him the surname "Bak," since the egg from which he had hatched was round like a gourd (the Korean word for which is *bak*), and the first name Hyeokgeose, meaning "he who makes the world bright."

The story of Bak Hyeokgeose, too, can be found in *Samguk sagi* and *Samguk yusa*. Like Baekje and Goguryeo, Saro gradually grew larger and stronger by conquering the small states around it. In 503, during the reign of King Jijeung, the name of the state was changed to "Silla (新羅)." This name was taken from a longer phrase, in Chinese, which means "achieving great deeds every day, expanding territory in all directions. [德業日新網羅四方]"

The Three Kingdoms period: a time of war

Goguryeo, Baekje and Silla all started out as small states then grew powerful by tirelessly conquering other countries around them. That's why the Three Kingdoms period is sometimes known as "the age of war."

 The names of Silla kings

The word normally used in Korean to mean king, "*wang*," is of Chinese origin. In Silla, before the word *wang* was introduced, titles used to mean king included *geoseogan*, *chachaung*, *isageum* and *maripgan*. Monarchs were not called XX-*wang* but XX-*maripgan* or XX-*isageum*.

The titles *geoseogan* and *chachaung* mean "bright sun" and "mudang" (a Korean spirit medium), respectively. Remember how I said that kings at that time also officiated at rites? Such figures were akin to *mudang*. It was believed that only Kings possessed the ability to communicate with the gods and officiate at rites, like a *mudang*.

The title *isageum* means "old person." The origin of the Korean term for somebody old comes from one that means "somebody with many teeth." For example, when Yuri and Talhae, the son and son-in-law, respectively, of King Namhae, were willing to cede the throne to each other, they both bit into a rice cake and Yuri, who left more teeth marks, became king first. *Maripgan*, meanwhile, means "supreme leader."

So when did Silla start using the word *wang*? Probably in 503, the same year that King Jijeung changed the name of his state from Saro to Silla.

First Goguryeo, then Baekje and finally Silla built the frameworks of states and accumulated ever more power.

War was the most effective shortcut to acquiring more land and manpower, the two most important commodities at a time when agriculture was the primary occupation. Nothing was better for farmers than fertile land, but this also called for people to work it.

Another important aspect of war was the question of how to integrate the peoples of conquered states and to win their hearts and minds. The solution to this problem lay in how the victorious side treated the ruling classes of the defeated state. In general, the latter were given high government positions and made to conform to the new order. People from the conquered state who did not belong to the ruling classes became commoners, untouchables or slaves.

The "Three Kingdoms period" we talk about today began when Goguryeo, Baekje and Silla had achieved supremacy. They then became fierce rivals. Sometimes, however, two of them would join forces in order to attack the third.

Gaya: land of iron

I almost forgot to mention Gaya. Around the time when Saro was rapidly expanding, several small states existed on the plains near the Nakdonggang River. These were known collectively as Byeonhan. It is here that the history of Gaya begins.

At the time, Gaya had no king and was ruled by nine leaders known as "*gan*." One day, a strange sound came from Gujibong Peak. When the nine *gan* gathered there, they heard a voice coming from an invisible source:

"Where am I?"

"Guji," they answered.

"The Heavens told me to found a state here and become its king. Dig down into the summit of the mountain while dancing and singing, 'Turtle, turtle, stick out your head. If you don't we'll cook and eat you.' Then, you will meet your new king."

The nine *gan* did as instructed, dancing and singing the song. Thereupon, a purple rope descended from the sky. At the end of it was a golden box wrapped in a red cloth. What do you think was in the box? Six golden eggs, as round as the sun.

After twelve days, a young child hatched from one of the eggs. They named him "Suro," reflecting the fact that he was the first to hatch. Suro became king and named his country "Gaya." Each of the five other babies hatched from eggs also become kings, making a total of six Gayas.

The story of King Suro is recorded in *Samguk yusa*. It mentions six Gayas - Geumgwan Gaya in Gimhae, Dae Gaya

Stele at Gujibong Peak
Gujibong Peak is located in Gimhae, Gyeongsangnam-do Province. The story of King Suro is set here.

Tombs in Jisan-dong, Goryeong
This area of Jisan-dong, Gyeongsangbuk-do Province, is home to around 200 large and small Gaya tombs on the upper slopes of its mountains.

in Goryeong, Ara Gaya in Haman, So Gaya in Goseong, Seongsan Gaya in Seongju and Goryeong Gaya in Hamchang - but in fact there were several other states, too.

Gaya was located in a region with plenty of high-grade iron ore. By exporting iron, it became very wealthy. Geumgwan Gaya, located where the Nakdonggang River flows into the sea at Gimhae, was able to sell iron to China and Japan thanks to its well-developed sea routes. The people of Gaya built a trading base as far away as Jeju-do and sailed to Kyushu in Japan to sell iron.

Gaya became a maritime superpower that dominated the

seas. Having grown rich by selling iron, it now developed a splendid culture of its own, much more sophisticated than that of Silla.

So why do people leave out Gaya and talk about Goguryeo, Baekje and Silla as the "Three Kingdoms?" Shouldn't it be four? The reason is that the various Gayas were conquered by Silla before they managed to unify into a single, powerful state. At first, the other Gayas came together under the leadership of Geumgwan Gaya and fought against Silla. After Geumgwan Gaya grew weak, they gathered under the leadership of Dae Gaya in Goryeong and joined forces with Baekje in opposition to Silla. The tide of war still ran against this alliance, however.

In 562, Dae Gaya finally collapsed in the face of a military attack led by Silla general Isabu. At this time, Ara Gaya in Haman and So Gaya in Goseong also fell. After some 500 years of continuous existence, the Gaya confederation now disappeared from history.

Gaya iron shaffron
Shaffrons such as this one were worn by horses for protection during battle.
–Pusan National University Museum

Armor and helmet
Just imagine a Gaya warrior on horseback, wearing these.
–Hangso Museum of Keimyung University

Gaya culture

The people of Gaya developed a very free and creative culture. The Gaya artifacts that remain with us today give a clear sense of this. Even the smallest piece of earthenware is full of unique Gaya style, totally different from that of Silla or Baekje. Could this be because Gaya engaged in maritime trade from early on? There is evidence that it enjoyed exchange with China and Japan. After Gaya fell, its beautiful culture was transmitted to Silla, along with the many former Gaya citizens who became part of the conquering state. Several famous Silla figures were actually former citizens of Gaya who moved to Silla after the defeat of the former, or their descendants. Kim Yusin, for example, widely known as Silla's most famous general, was descended from Gaya royalty. Renowned scholar Gang Su and musician U Reuk, who invented the *gayageum* (Korean zither), also came from Gaya.

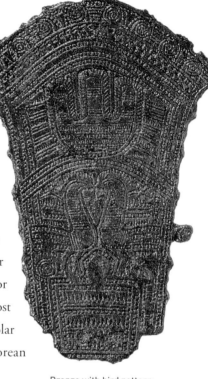

Bronze with bird pattern
Two birds are engraved in the middle of this bronze. The people of Gaya believed that birds led the souls of the deceased up to Heaven.
− National Museum of Korea

− Gimhae National Museum

Cup with triangular perforations

Cup separated from holder

• Various forms of Gaya earthenware

Gaya earthenware comes in a wide variety of forms, including those of wagon wheels, houses and so on.

Wagon wheel-shaped
earthenware vessel
– Jinju National Museum

Straw sandal-shaped
earthenware vessel
– Busan Museum

Duck-shaped
earthenware vessel
– National Museum of Korea

Earthenware vessel in the shape
of a warrior on horseback
– Gyeongju National Museum

Bird-shaped
earthenware vessel
– Bokcheon Museum

CHAPTER 7

Goguryeo: a Northeast Asian superpower

Gwanggaeto the Great was a brave general and outstanding strategist. He led his own armies from battle to battle and was so brave that his enemies would give up as soon as they heard he was on his way.

Gwanggaeto invaded Baekje and took control of the area around the Imjingang River. He then turned north and attacked the Khitans, before heading northwest and penetrating into China as far as Shanxi Province.

Paleolithic period
Stone tools

Neolithic period
Earthenware made from clay; agriculture begins

Gojoseon founded
Dangun Wanggeom foundation myth

Shall I start today's letter with the story of Prince Hodong of Goguryeo and Princess Nangnang?

Hodong and Nangnang were in love. The prince's father, King Daemusin, wanted to attack Nangnang but was wavering because of Jamyeonggo and Ppulpiri, a mysterious drum and a horn, respectively, that beat and played themselves to warn of coming enemy attacks. When he saw his father hesitating, Hodong wrote to Princess Nangnang warning her of the attack and asking her to stop Jamyeonggo from beating.

How must Princess Nangnang have felt? Doing as Hodong asked would place her own country in danger, but refusing would endanger Hodong himself. Finally, she sneaked into the armoury, slashed Jamyeonggo with a knife and smashed Ppulpiri. Goguryeo then attacked. When Choe Ri, king of Nangnang, learned what had happened, he cut down the princess with a single sword stroke.

This story dates from the time when Goguryeo was engaged in a series of endless wars with its neighbors and expanding its territory. Let's take a closer look at this process of expansion.

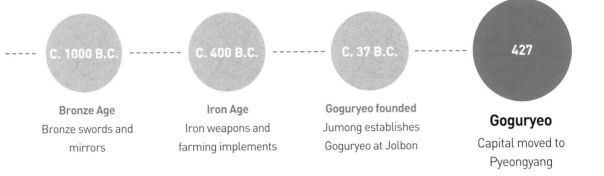

C. 1000 B.C.	**C. 400 B.C.**	**C. 37 B.C.**	**427**
Bronze Age	**Iron Age**	**Goguryeo founded**	**Goguryeo**
Bronze swords and mirrors	Iron weapons and farming implements	Jumong establishes Goguryeo at Jolbon	Capital moved to Pyeongyang

The story of Prince Hodong and Princess Nangnang is set at a time when various countries fought against each other without respite. Winning wars, expanding territory and gaining people meant creating a stronger state, bringing riches and power. Princess Nangnang was sacrificed in the process of Goguryeo's conquering of neighboring states. And she was far from the only one. Though we no longer know their names, there would have been countless such victims with similarly tragic stories.

Hodong must have been heartbroken despite his victory, don't you think? Perhaps because of this, the Prince also met a tragic end a few months after the death of Princess Nangnang. His stepmother, the queen consort, afraid that he would become heir to the throne instead of her own

Nangnang
What kind of state was Nangnang? Was it the same Nangnang as one of the four commanderies established by Han after it had defeated Gojoseon? Though their names are the same, scholars claim that the Nangnang in the story of Hodong and the princess was not the Han commandery but a different entity. It seems to have been a small state that spun off from Nangnang Commandery.

son, began to slander him. Without evening trying to defend himself, Hodong committed suicide. Perhaps he wanted to be reunited with Princess Nangnang, who had lost her own life because of him.

Gwanggaeto: Great king and conqueror of Northeast Asia

400 years after the heartbreaking story of Prince Hodong and Princess Nangnang, Goguryeo had become a powerful state by gradually increasing its strength. It now dominated Northeast Asia, possessing a huge territory that stretched from the Imjingang River all the way to Manchuria. At this time, it was ruled by a king known as Gwanggaeto the Great.

The Gwanggaeto Stele is located in Taiwang Township, Ji'an City, Jilin Province in today's Manchuria. This is where the Goguryeo capital of Gungnaeseong once stood. Jumong's son, King Yuri, had the capital moved from Jolbon to Gungnaeseong. The deep mountains in this area protected the city from enemy attacks, while the forests and rivers were rich in deer, reindeer, fish and turtles and the land was suitable for farming.

Also known as the "King Hotae Stele," the Gwanggaeto Stele was created in 414 by King Jangsu, son of Gwanggaeto the Great, in praise of his father's achievements. "Gwanggaeto the Great" is a posthumous title, shorted

Gwanggaeto Stele
This stele is made from a huge piece of granite, the four sides of which are filled with 1,775 Chinese characters. Because the stone was not polished but used in its natural state, the surface of the stele is uneven. It is 6.4 meters tall and weighs 37 tonnes.

from a much longer one: "Gukgangsang Gwanggaetogyeong Pyeong Anhotaewang." Gwanggaeto's real name, meanwhile, was "Damdeok."

Shanchengxia Goguryeo tombs
These tombs are located in Ji'an in today's Jilin Province, Manchuria. The wide field is filled with more than 1,500 tombs. On top of the mountain behind the field is Wandou-shancheng Mountain Fortress; this is why the tombs are known as "Shanchengxia," meaning "below the mountain fortress."

When Damdeok was still crown prince, his father, King Gogugyang, gave him a sword and spoke to him:

"This sword is a treasure that has been passed down since the time of King Jumong, founder of Goguryeo. Take good care of it and ensure that you do your utmost to prepare to lead the country."

Crown prince Damdeok became king as soon as his father died. It was 391, and he was eighteen years old. At this time, China was divided into several states that were at war with each other and had no time to take any notice of Goguryeo. Taking advantage of this opportunity, Gwanggaeto the Great did everything in his power to expand his own territory.

He began by attacking Baekje, to the south. Gwanggaeto the Great was a brave general and outstanding strategist. He led his own armies from battle to battle and was so brave that his enemies would give up as soon as they heard he was on his way.

Gwanggaeto invaded Baekje and took control of the

Taewangneung
Surely the tomb of Gwanggaeto the Great must be located somewhere near the Gwanggaeto Stele? Actually, we still don't know for sure where his grave is. Some claim he is buried at a tomb called Taewangneung; others that he lies in one known as Janggunchong. Taewangneung is a stone mound tomb that measures sixty-six meters along each side. Seen from a distance, it looks more like a hill than a tomb.

Warrior on horseback
This image is of a gallant Goguryeo warrior wearing a hat decorated with feathers and galloping along on horseback. It is a fragment of a mural from Ssangyeongchong Tomb, taken away by the Japanese during the colonial period.
– National Museum of Korea

area around the Imjingang River. He then turned north and attacked the Khitans, before heading northwest and penetrating into China as far as Shanxi Province.

Feeling threatened by Goguryeo's expansion, the Chinese state of Later Yan seized an opportunity to attack while Gwanggaeto was on an expedition to Silla. The Goguryeo king responded by crossing the Liaohe River, invading Later Yan and taking Sujun Fortress. This was former Gojoseon territory. The Liaodong and Liaoxi areas, taken long ago from Gojoseon by Han, had been recovered after 700 years. Gwanggaeto also won control of Buyeo and the Mohe people.

Goguryeo was now a powerful state that reached from the Amur River in Manchuria to the north, the Imjingang River, near Seoul, to the south, Russia's Primorsky Krai to the east and the Liaohe River to the west. At this time, it was the greatest kingdom in Northeast Asia.

After becoming king, Gwanggaeto the Great spent around twenty years practically living on the battlefield, before dying at the age of just forty.

King Jangsu pushes back Baekje

King Jangsu, successor of Gwanggaeto the

Great, moved the Goguryeo capital from Gungnaeseong, by the Amnokgang River, to the banks of the Daedonggang River, where Pyeongyang now stands. He put all of his effort into ruling the territory expanded by his father, while working hard to establish diplomatic ties with various states in China by dispatching Goguryeo envoys.

Next, King Jangsu attacked Baekje. At this time, the southwestern state was ruled by a king named Gaero. In the Goguryeo attack, Baekje lost Hanseong and the Hangang River, areas it had defended for almost 500 years, and was forced to relocate its capital to Ungjin (now Gongju, in Chungcheongnam-do Province), further south.

Losing the Hangang meant forfeiting the lead in the competition between the Three Kingdoms. As I'll mention again later, the river was a major transportation route that enabled easy contact by sea with China; controlling it was important enough to determine victory or defeat.

In any case, the Hangang had now fallen from Baekje hands into those of Goguryeo; the latter had reached its zenith, its territory larger than ever before. Unlike his father, King Jangsu lived a long life, eventually

Khitan people
The Khitan were a nomadic Mongolic people that lived around the upper reaches of the Liaohe River. In 907, they founded their own state and called it Liao. Liao invaded Korea during the Goryeo period but was repelled thanks to the efforts of figures such as Gang Gam-chan and Seo Hui.

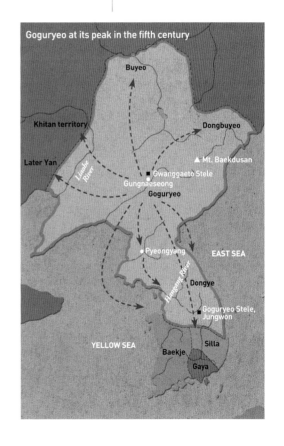

Goguryeo at its peak in the fifth century

dying at the age of ninety-eight.

Meanwhile, Baekje and Silla entered an alliance in order to survive against their fearsome northern neighbor. This was known as the "Naje Alliance," combining parts of the names of Silla and Baekje.

Around 100 years later the Hangang changed hands once again, from Goguryeo to Silla. The reason competition to win this river was so intense was that controlling it was the only way for a state to enjoy the height of success.

Goguryeo Stele, Jungwon
This stele was erected during the reign of King Jangsu of Goguryeo. It tells us that his country's territory extended as far south as the Namhangang River in the fifth century. It was discovered in Jungwon in today's Chungcheongbuk-do Province, hence its name.

The battles of Salsu River and Ansiseong Fortress

Goguryeo fought a succession of battles against China's Sui and Tang dynasties for around 70 years. Sui and Tang were major powers that unified China. What would have happened if Goguryeo had been defeated by them? Perhaps the Korean Peninsula would have become Chinese territory.

In the summer of 612, Sui Emperor Yangdi invaded Goguryeo with an army of one million men. General Eulji Mundeok of Goguryeo pretended to lose battles and retreated in order to tire out the enemy. When the Sui forces had drawn near to Pyeongyangseong Fortress, Eulji Mundeok sent a poem to enemy commander Yu Zhongwen.

Your otherworldly resourcefulness penetrates the heavens.

The Battle of Salsu River
Not even a mighty Sui army of one million men proved capable of beating Goguryeo.

Goguryeo warriors
in armor
This tomb mural depicts
Goguryeo warriors. Their
bodies are clad in armor
and they're wearing
helmets. Don't these
fighters, who beat back
attacks from Sui and Tang,
cut imposing figures?

Your exquisite machinations show your mastery of the earth.

Your victory has proved you eminently meritorious.

I hope you may now feel satisfied and end this war.

When they read this poem, the Sui army and Yu Zhongwen began to retreat in the belief that they had saved face. But when they were around half way across the Salsu (now Cheongcheongang) River, Goguryeo forces launched an attack from behind. The waters of the river turned blood-red in an instant and the Sui army was all but annihilated. This event is known as the Battle of Salsu River. Emperor Yangdi attacked Goguryeo a few more times after this, but failed each time; this merely served to increase the resentment among his war-tired people. Eventually, the Sui dynasty fell and the Tang dynasty emerged in its place.

In 645, thirty-three years after the Battle of Salsu River, Tang Emperor Taizong led an army of 100,000 men in an attack on

Goguryeo. The Tang army laid siege to Ansiseong Fortress on the Liaodong Peninsula. This fortress was small but highly important, as its loss would mean that Liaodong fell entirely into the hands of Tang.

Ansiseong did not fall easily, however. Under the leadership of Yang Manchun, its governor, the commoners and soldiers in the castle came together as one and fought. Taizong tried everything he could think of, but failed to take the castle. In the end, all he could do was give the order to retreat. After eighty-eight days, the Goguryeo forces defending Ansiseong were finally victorious.

 ## Eulji Mundeok and Yang Manchun

Eulji Mundeok disappears completely from the history books after the Battle of Salsu River. Some say this is because he died suddenly following the battle; we cannot now know for sure.

Yang Manchun is not even recorded properly by name in history books. *Samguk sagi* claims that the name of the governor of

The battle of Ansiseong Fortress.
-The War Memorial of Korea

Ansiseong Fortress is not known. The reason we know about Yang today is that his name is recorded in *Yeolha ilgi* ("Jehol Diary") by Joseon scholar Park Jiwon and in *Dongchundang seonsaeng byeoljip* ("Anthology of the Writings of Song Jungil"). It seems his name was passed down through the generations by word of mouth. One story even claims that Yang Manchun shot Tang Emperor Taizong in the eye with an arrow.

The riddle of the Gwanggaeto Stele

Some Japanese scholars claim that an institution called "Imna Japanese Headquarters" once existed on the Korean Peninsula. According to this argument, Japan expanded into the region of Gaya, in the south of the peninsula, from the late-4th to mid-6th century, establishing a Japanese command post and controlling both Baekje and Silla. As evidence for this claim, scholars cite a single line from the Gwanggaeto Stele. The Chinese characters in it are a bit hard, but let's have a look anyway:

倭以辛卯年來渡海破百殘□□□羅以爲臣民

You'll notice that three characters are missing: these have been erased and are now illegible. So what were the missing characters, and how should the three characters, "渡海破" be understood? Their interpretation has the potential to change the entire meaning of the line.

Japanese scholars interpret the line to their own advantage, translating it as, "Wa [Japan] crossed the sea in the year Sinmyo (391), defeated Baekje and Silla, and made them its vassals." They cite this as conclusive evidence for the existence of Imna Japanese Headquarters.

A rubbing taken from the Gwanggaeto Stele

At that time, however, there was no Japanese political entity powerful enough to be called a state, and Baekje and Silla were both far more advanced than Japan. The interpretation offered by Japanese scholars is therefore at odds with reality.

This has even prompted others to claim that this part of the stele was forged by the Japanese during the colonial period. What's even more important is the fact that the purported existence of Imna Japanese Headquarters was later used as a claim to justify Japan's colonial ambitions. This argument holds that since Korea was controlled by Japan in the distant past, it was natural for it to become a Japanese colony even in the early 20th century. Some Japanese school textbooks still mention Imna Japanese Headquarters, while the mystery of the Gwanggaeto Stele itself has yet to be solved.

The Gwanggaeto Stele today
A pavilion with glass walls has now been built around the stele to protect it.

CHAPTER 8

Baekje,
land of cultural
refinement

Large grain harvests reaped from their wide plains provided the people of Baekje with lives of plenty. In the past, just as today, material abundance provides the foundations for flourishing arts and culture. Baekje's elegant and sophisticated culture can be regarded as the fruit of its natural environment and material wealth.

Its active overseas trade also gave Baekje a decisive edge over Goguryeo and Silla.

TIME LINE

427

Goguryeo
Capital moved to
Pyeongyang

475

Baekje
Capital moved to Ungjin

527

Silla
Ichadon put to death;
Buddhism officially
recognized

When we hear the name Baekje, we normally think of Buyeo and Gongju, its two capitals. Gongju was capital of Baekje for sixty-three years and Buyeo for 122. But there's another city that was capital of Baekje for much longer than both of these: Seoul.

Seoul was capital of Baekje for 493 years after the founding of the state. This period, however, is shrouded in mystery. Today, it's as if we have forgotten three quarters of Baekje's entire history and know only the remaining quarter.

As I said in my last letter, by around the fifth century, Goguryeo was the most powerful state in Northeast Asia. Totally confident in its power, it now proudly controlled more territory than at any time since its founding. But Baekje, its rival, was also quite a force to be reckoned with.

Today, let's go back to the time Baekje abandoned its capital, and was pushed south. It was 475 and King Jangsu of Goguryeo was attacking Seoul.

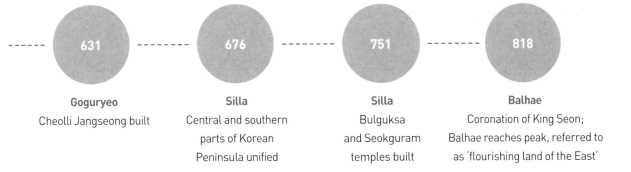

631	676	751	818
Goguryeo	**Silla**	**Silla**	**Balhae**
Cheolli Jangseong built	Central and southern parts of Korean Peninsula unified	Bulguksa and Seokguram temples built	Coronation of King Seon; Balhae reaches peak, referred to as 'flourishing land of the East'

King Jangsu of Goguryeo decided he could no longer put off attacking Baekje. News reached him that King Gaero of Baekje had sent a letter to China's Northern Wei Dynasty asking it to send troops to help with an attack on Goguryeo. King Jangsu rapidly began his invasion. The year was 475 and he was now eighty-two.

Sweeping forcefully down the peninsula, Goguryeo's troops left Baekje overwhelmed. Finally, they laid to siege to the Baekje capital, Hanseong (today's Seoul). This city consisted of a northern and a southern fortress: the former fell after seven days. Just before the siege began, King Gaero sent his younger brother to Silla, then an ally of Baekje, to ask for help.

You'll remember how I told you that Baekje and Silla had

Northern Wei
This state, founded by a clan of the Xianbei people, existed in a northern region of China from 386 to 534.

Three-legged cauldron
This cauldron was excavated from Pungnaptoseong. It has three legs and a long handle in the shape of a dragon's neck and head. It was used for heating liquids such as wine.
– National Museum of Korea

Pungnaptoseong Fortress
This fortress is believed, together with Mongchontoseong, to have formed Baekje's first capital. When land in Pungnap-dong in eastern Seoul's Gangdong-gu District was dug up in order to build apartments, a large number of ancient remains and artifacts was discovered. Pungnaptoseong is nine meters tall and a total of four kilometers long.

formed an alliance called Naje and promised to help each other in the event of a Goguryeo invasion.

But Baekje's southern fortress, too, fell to Goguryeo before the troops sent by Silla to help its ally had even arrived. King Gaero was captured, taken to Acha Sanseong Mountain Fortress and killed. His queen consort and all of his sons were put to death, too. Jangsu made his way leisurely back to Goguryeo, taking some 8,000 Baekje citizens with him.

Returning too late, Gaero's younger brother quickly took the throne, becoming King Munju, and attempted to pick up the pieces of his state. He moved his capital far to the south, to the place we now know as Gongju, in Chungcheongnam-do Province.

In search of Hanseong, capital of Baekje

Hanseong, the Baekje capital that fell to Goguryeo, was located near Seoul's Hangang River. But you will recall how I described the way Onjo, the founder of Baekje, built his capital at a place called Wiryeseong. So are Wiryeseong and Hanseong the same place or not? Different people make a variety of claims, but I think they are the same place.

In which case, where exactly was Hanseong or Wiryeseong located?

Some say it was at Mongchontoseong Fortress, now in the Olympic Park in Seoul's Songpa-gu District; others, that it was at Pungnaptoseong Fortress, a little further to the north. Still others believe it was at Iseongsanseong Mountain Fortress in Hanam, Gyeong-gi-do. Or that Pungnaptoseong was the northern fortress of Hanseong, which fell to Goguryeo after seven days, and Mongchontoseong was the southern fortress at which King Gaero was captured.

Now do you know what I mean when I say the history of Baekje is shrouded in mystery? We don't even know for sure where its capital of some 500 years was located!

In any case, the death of Gaero and the fall of Hanseong meant that Baekje lost control of the Hangang area.

Until then, the Hangang had functioned as a lifeline for Baekje, playing a vital role in the flourishing of the state. Losing the river was a huge blow.

Mongchontoseong
and its wooden barricade
Mongchontoseong is built from six or seven meters of earth piled on top of a natural hill. This was surrounded by a stout wooden barricade and a moat, leaving the fortress solidly defended. The wooden barricade in the lower photo is a recent reconstruction; all that remains of the original is its position.

Was King Gaero really a tyrant?

The fall of Baekje's capital is widely attributed to the fact that King Gaero was an inept politician and a greedy and brutal man. *Samguk sagi* cites stories such as The "Tale of Domi's Wife" and "The Tale of Dorim" as evidence of this.

Domi's wife was famous for her beauty. When rumors of her reached the ears of King Gaero, he began to lust after her. He summoned Domi, tortured him, plucked both of his eyes out and sent him away. But Domi's wife used her wits to escape Gaero and flee. She found her husband and went to live with him in faraway Goguryeo.

Dorim was a Buddhist monk from Goguryeo and an outstanding *baduk* (*go*) player. King Jangsu sent Dorim as a spy to get close to King Gaero. Gaero loved *baduk* and played it every day with Dorim while neglecting to govern his country.

Dorim incited Gaero to build himself a magnificent palace, saying that the current one was too modest for a king of such dignity. Gaero did as Dorim suggested and began work on a new palace for himself, which ended up turning public sentiment against him.

King Jangsu took advantage of this situation to attack Baekje; Gaero ended up losing both his country and his life.

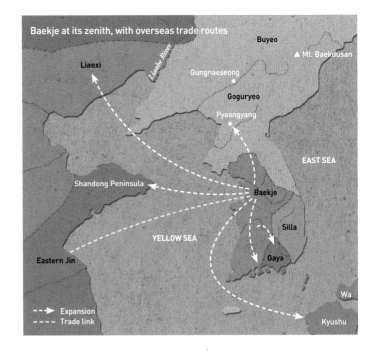

Baekje at its zenith, with overseas trade routes

Both tales portray Gaero as an incompetent and horribly greedy king. In reality, however, he was not all that useless or brutal.

A highly ambitious individual, Gaero wanted to secure himself large amounts of power. While establishing close ties with China and Japan, he pursued a brand of politics in which the monarch played a central role.

The king's oppressive, monarch-centered policies also created a faction opposed to him. Jaejeunggeollu and Goimannyeon, two figures who played a leading role in the eventual capture of Gaero, were originally from Baekje but had defected to Goguryeo. Perhaps they had been part of the opposing faction that was unhappy with Gaero's policies.

Seosan Buddha Triad
The beaming faces of the Buddhas in this photo are sometimes referred to as "the smile of Baekje." Carved into the side of a large rock, they are located in a valley in Seosan, Chungcheongnam-do Province, on an old route from Baekje to China. Would the people of Baekje have had such radiant, gentle smiles as these Buddhas?
– Buyeo National Museum

It strikes me that the tales of Domi's wife and Dorim were inflated or enhanced versions of reality, created after Gaero's death to damage his reputation and portray him as a terrible king.

Sophisticated culture:
the fruit of material abundance

Baekje boasted a highly sophisticated culture. It left behind the most elegant and refined artifacts among the Three Kingdoms.

Baekje was also located on the flattest territory of the Korean Peninsula. The nearby Yellow Sea, moreover, offered easy access to China and Japan.

With its wide plains, Baekje's agriculture - particularly rice cultivation - developed early. It also created irrigation facilities, an essential part of rice cultivation, building dykes and creating reservoirs to allow the use of water whenever it was needed. Baekje scholars mastered astrometeorology for predicting the weather.

Large grain harvests reaped from their wide plains provided the people of Baekje with lives of plenty. In the past, just as today, material abundance provides the foundations for flourishing arts and culture. Baekje's elegant and sophisticated culture can be regarded as the fruit of its natural environment and material wealth.

Its active overseas trade also gave Baekje a decisive edge over Goguryeo and Silla. It soon developed ties with several Chinese states and began to absorb Chinese influence. Perhaps this is what gave Baekje culture its international character.

Baekje developed a flourishing Buddhist culture after adopting Buddhism from China. It also embraced Confucianism and turned out scholars well-versed in Confucian classics, known as *ogyeong baksa* ("savants of the Five Classics"); preeminent among them was Goheung. On the orders of the king, Go compiled *Seogi*, Baekje's first history book.

Some claim that *Seogi* is not a book title but just a term that means "a written record." Even if *Seogi* is not an actual title, I think there can be no doubt that Go Heung, a scholar during the reign of King Geunchogo, wrote a history of his country.

In addition to *ogyeong baksa* were other types of savant specializing in various technologies. Specialist roof tile manufacturers were known as *wa baksa* ("master tile makers") and specialist metalworkers as *noban baksa* ("master of casting the metal decorations at the tops of stupas"). One *noban baksa* by the name of Baek Maesun

Patterned brick
This square brick is decorated with a carved pattern depicting a beautiful landscape inhabited by fairies. It was discovered in Buyeo, Chungcheongnam-do Province.
– Buyeo National Museum

King Geunchogo
The 13th king of Baekje, Geunchogo ruled from 346 to 375. He was a conqueror comparable to Gwanggaeto the Great of Goguryeo, extending Baekje's territory into today's Jeolla-do region by defeating Mahan, and advancing northwards almost all the way to Pyeongyang and killing King Gogugwon of Goguryeo in battle.

Baekje envoys to China
The picture above is a detail depicting a Baekje envoy in a sixth-century work titled *Liang zhigongtu* ("Portraits of Periodical offering of Liang"). Baekje, Goguryeo and Silla all enjoyed active exchange with China. On the right are envoys from the Three Kingdoms - Goguryeo, Baekje and Silla, in order from the left - as illustrated in another Chinese work, *Wanghuitu* ("Picture of a Gathering of Kings"), which dates from the seventh century.

Kettle with chicken's head spout
This kettle was excavated from the site of the former Baekje capital, Ungjin.
– National Museum of Korea

went to Japan and worked actively there.

Other Baekje craftmen specialized in building Buddhist temples. These were known as *josagong* or *sagong*. Specialist manufacturers of Buddha statues were called *jobulgong* and specialist painters *hwagong*.

Famous Baekje craftmen traveled by invitation to other countries. The nine-story pagoda at Hwangnyongsa Temple in Silla was built by Abiji, a specialist invited from Baekje. Seokgatap and Dabotap, the two famous stupas at Bulguksa Temple in Silla, were built by Asadal, another Baekje craftsman. Baekje scholars, monks and craftmen also crossed the sea to Japan, where they passed on their country's advanced culture and arts.

Baekje's revival

After relocating its capital to Ungjin, Baekje calmly set about making a comeback. Hanseong had been reduced to ashes and King Gaero was dead, but the country had not collapsed completely. Twenty-six years later, it finally regained its former vitality. At this time it was ruled by King Muryeong, followed by his son, King Seong.

Muryeong was tall, handsome and generous, traits that made him popular among his people. He brought political stability to Baekje, putting at ease the peasants who had previously fled in the face of war and starvation so that they returned and started farming once again.

Muryeong's successor, King Seong, moved the Baekje capital to Sabiseong Fortress, the place we know today as Buyeo in Chungcheongnam-do. Having relocated his capital and organized his country, Seong now set about trying to fulfil a long-held desire by attacking Goguryeo. What he wanted, of course, was to win back the Hangang River.

King Seong formed an allied army with King Jinheung of Silla and attacked Goguryeo, eventually winning back the area around the Hangang. This happened some seventy years after Baekje lost the same territory under King Gaero.

Gilt-bronze incense burner
When incense was lit and placed in this burner, its scent would diffuse through holes in the lid. The people of Baekje believed that burning incense not only got rid of bad smells but conveyed prayers to the gods. This magnificent item is testimony to the standard of Baekje art.
–Buyeo National Museum

Restored burial chamber in the tomb of King Muryeong

Baekje's happiness proved short-lived, however. This time, it lost the Hangang to Silla. How did this happen? I'll have a chance to tell you about that in more detail another time.

After briefly faltering, Baekje regained its strength under King Mu. During the reigns of Seong and Mu, it enjoyed a mature and sophisticated culture and a lot of power. But

The newly discovered tomb of King Muryeong
This tomb was rediscovered in July, 1971, revealing itself to the world for the first time in 1,500 years. Those entering it were immediately confronted by a stone animals, blocking the way. In front of the beast were two square memorial stones, side by side, upon which a bundle of coins had been placed. Carved on the memorial stones were inscriptions indicating that the tomb contained King Muryeong and his queen consort. The bundle of coins was probably meant to help the deceased on their way to the afterlife.

under King Uija, son of King Mu, the country was brought down by a military alliance between Silla and Tang.

Who made these huge jar coffins?

Large numbers of jar coffins, consisting of two huge jars fitted together, have been discovered at Naju and Yeongam in Jeollanam-do Province, where the Yeongsangang River flows. These were not made by the people of Baekje who, like their Goguryeo neighbors, made tombs by building piles of stones. Who, then, made them?

Baekje began near the Hangang River before extending its power southwards. It reached as far south as Naju and Yeongam around the fourth century, during the reign of King Geunchogo. It looks, then, as if the jar coffins were made by settlers in these areas before the arrival of Baekje. These were none other than the people of Mahan. The area around the Yeongsangang was the last bastion of native Mahan culture. Its inhabitants also engaged in trade with Japan. The earthenware items buried in tombs here are highly similar to Japanese artifacts.

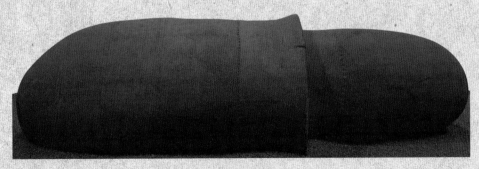

Jar coffin
This coffin was discovered near the Yeongsangang River.

King Mu and Princess Seonhwa

Before King Mu of Baekje acceded to the throne, he lived a life of poverty with his single mother, barely scraping a living by foraging for and selling yams. He therefore acquired the name Seodong, meaning "boy who digs up yams." Yams, known as *ma* in Korean, are similar to potatoes.

Gungnamji Pond, Buyeo
This pond was created at the time of King Mu of Baekje; its name means "pond to the south of the palace." It's a beautiful spot, where the refined culture of Baekje seems to live on.

After hearing a rumor about the beauty of Princess Seonhwa, third daughter of King Jinpyeong of Silla, Seodong made his way there and began giving out free yams to the children while teaching them a song. The song, which the children then went around singing, described how Princess Seonhwa secretly met Seodong every night:

Princess Seonhwa
Got married in secret.
Every night, she sneaks into Seodong's room
And stays in his arms till morning

When King Jinpyeong heard the song he hit the roof and banished the princess. Seodong, who was waiting for Seonhwa on her way into exile, confessed the truth to her and went with her to Baekje.

This story is recorded in *Samguk yusa*. One aspect of it is worth thinking about: if Princess Seonhwa was the third daughter of King Jinpyeong, that makes her the younger sister of the famous Queen Seondeok of Silla. Surprisingly, though, there is no word of Seonhwa in *Samguk sagi* . The only two daughters of King Jinpyeong listed in this history are Queen Seondeok and Princess Cheonmyeong. During Jinpyeong's reign, moreover, Baekje and Silla were on extremely bad terms and often went to war with each other. A marriage between King Mu and Princess Seonhwa at a time like this would have been a very significant event, worthy of being recorded in history books without question. Still, *Samguk sagi* says nothing about their union at all. Isn't that strange?

This story in *Samguk yusa* was originally an explanation as to how the Buddhist temple Mireuksa in Iksan, Jeollabuk-do Province, was founded. According to the tale, King Mu had the temple built at the request of Princess Seonhwa. He also intended to move his capital to Iksan.

King Mu came to the throne with the support of the people of Iksan. Some scholars therefore speculate the Seonhwa may have been the daughter of a powerful Iksan family or of a member of the Baekje royal family or aristocracy. As the story was passed on orally from one person to the next, Seonhwa was transformed into a Silla princess. What do you think? Who was Princess Seonhwa? Try to imagine for yourself.

Sarira enshrinement record and bottle found in a stone pagoda at Mireuksaji Temple Site
In January 2009, during repairs to the remaining stone pagoda at Mireuksaji, a bottle containing sarira and an enshrinement record with details of the building of the pagoda were discovered. The record reads that Mireuksa Temple was established by "the queen of Baekje, daughter of Jwapyeong Sataek Jeokdeok." Jwapyeong was a noble rank in Baekje, which makes it clear that the founder of Mireuksa was not a Silla princess.
−National Research Institute of Cultural Heritage

CHAPTER 9

Buddhism, key to the culture of the Three Kingdoms

After wracking his brains for some time, the king had a sudden stroke of inspiration. He realized that what was needed at this point was a new way of thinking - a new religion. He now believed that he needed a new faith that was both novel and capable of suppressing Silla's indigenous beliefs; one that would silence the country's aristocracy and force it into submission.

TIME LINE -------- 427 -------- 475 -------- 527 --------

Goguryeo
Capital moved to Pyeongyang

Baekje
Capital moved to Ungjin

Silla
Ichadon put to death; Buddhism officially recognized

Cathedrals are among the most common cultural and historical sites in Europe. The reason there are so many of them across the continent is that Christianity was the official religion there for around 1,000 years. This religion is deeply rooted in the lives and thoughts of Europeans, which is why it's hard to understand Western culture properly without some knowledge of it.

I think the position of Buddhism in Korean culture is similar to that of Christianity in the West. After first arriving on the peninsula during the Three Kingdoms period, it became the state-promoted religion for roughly 1,000 years, until the end of the Goryeo period, exerting huge influence on Korean history and culture.

Now do you understand why the cultural and historic sites most commonly found in Korea are Buddhist temples, stupas, Buddha statues and other places associated with Buddhism? This is what makes it the key to understanding the culture of the Three Kingdoms.

Well then - today, let's go back to the time when Buddhism first arrived.

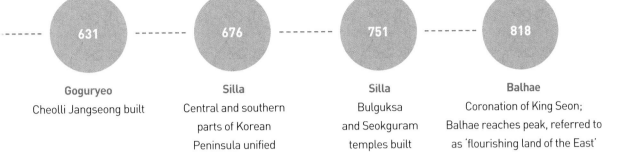

631	676	751	818
Goguryeo	**Silla**	**Silla**	**Balhae**
Cheolli Jangseong built	Central and southern parts of Korean Peninsula unified	Bulguksa and Seokguram temples built	Coronation of King Seon; Balhae reaches peak, referred to as 'flourishing land of the East'

Buddhism came to Goguryeo in 372, during the reign of King Sosurim. It was transmitted from the Chinese state of Former Qin by the monk Shundao, who brought Buddhist images and sutras. Twelve years later, during the reign of King Chimnyu in 384, the monk Malananta traveled to Baekje from Eastern Jin and introduced Buddhism. Thus, the royal households of Goguryeo and Baekje had officially recognized Buddhism by the later part of the fourth century, but only after the faith had already reached parts of the population in both states.

Not all of the Three Kingdoms adopted Buddhism in the exactly the same way. Goguryeo and Baekje accepted it without too much friction, but Silla still held strong indigenous beliefs that had been passed down

Gilt-bronze standing Buddha with the inscription from the seventh year of the 'Yeonga era' - front and back views
This Goguryeo Buddha statue was discovered at Hachon-ri in Daeui-myeon, Uiryeong-gun, Gyeongsangnam-do Province - Silla territory. It is testimony to the close cultural ties that existed between Goguryeo and Silla. On its reverse are carved forty-seven Chinese characters that explain the statue's origins: in the seventh year of the "Yeonga era," forty people in the eastern temple of Nangnang in Goguryeo decided to get together and make 1,000 Buddhist statues; this was the twenty-ninth among them.
– National Museum of Korea

from long ago. In the face of strong opposition from the Silla aristocracy, Buddhism did not achieve easy recognition. It was only with the death of a man named Ichadon that Silla, too, came to officially acknowledge Buddhism.

Let me start by telling you the story of Ichadon.

Ichadon dies for King Beopheung

King Beopheung of Silla was in a quandary. He needed a way of suppressing members of the aristocracy that were opposing him in every matter, but couldn't think of one.

After wracking his brains for some time, the king had a sudden stroke of inspiration. He realized that what was needed at this point was a new way of thinking - a new religion. He now believed that he needed a new faith that was both novel and capable of suppressing Silla's indigenous beliefs; one that would silence the country's aristocracy and force it into submission. By that time, it had already been 150 years since neighboring Goguryeo and Baekje adopted Buddhism from China and recognized it as a state religion. Only Silla had not accepted the faith, due to opposition from its aristocracy.

Silla's nobility still insisted on the country's age-old beliefs in worshipping the gods of Heaven and Earth and the spirits of their ancestors. These traditions had been handed down all the way from Gojoseon, making it very difficult to change them overnight.

Buddhism, however, was very useful for enhancing the authority of kings. At this time, Chinese emperors claimed themselves to be Buddhas, rendering their authority sacred.

Beopheung considered this: since the Buddha was a unique, absolute being who transcended all else, a king who served the Buddha would have good reason to suppress all those who challenged him. It was clear, however, that this plan would meet with a considerable backlash from the aristocracy. It was then that a court official named Ichadon, who had noticed the king agonizing over this deep dilemma, secretly went to speak to him.

"I will gladly give my own life," he said. "Sacrifice me in order to suppress the others."

Ichadon went to Cheongyeongnim Forest, saying that he had received royal orders to build a Buddhist temple, and began chopping down trees. Cheongyeongnim was a sacred forest in which rites were held in honor of the god of heaven. The idea of building a Buddhist temple there was enough to give the aristocracy a fit. Furious nobles descended upon the royal palace. The king, however, claimed to know nothing about the affair and ordered that Ichadon be arrested. Ichadon, meanwhile, claimed to have planned the whole thing by himself. All of this had already been arranged in

Memorial to the martyrdom of Ichadon This memorial stone pays tribute to the death of Ichadon. The carving shows white milk spouting up out of his neck, and flowers raining down all around. Ichadon's death illustrates just how hard it was for Buddhism to be accepted in Silla. He was a loyal retainer who volunteered his own life in the fight between King Beopheung, who wanted to use Buddhism to enhance his royal authority, and the Silla aristocrats who opposed him.
–Gyeongju National Museum

Five-storey stone pagoda, Jeongnimsa Temple
This pagoda remains at the site of Jeongnimsa Temple in Buyeo, the last Baekje capital. It exemplifies the refinement and elegance of Baekje. The four faces of the lowest storey are filled with an engraved message under the title "Daedang pyeong baekje bimyeong" ("Inscription telling how the Great Tang defeated Baekje"). This was carved by Tang forces on the pagoda as a record of Tang's victory over Baekje.

secret by Ichadon and Beopheung.

The king gave the order for Ichadon's head to be chopped off. At this point, according to *Samguk yusa*, not red blood but "white milk shot upwards to a height of several meters, the heavens turned black, the Earth trembled and flowers rained down from the sky."

Beopheung now spoke menacingly to the assembled aristocrats, telling them he would have every last one of them executed for the crime of groundlessly defying the king. The aristocrats prostrated themselves before him and begged for their lives. The king then spoke once again, in a solemn tone:

"I'll forgive you just this once. But since Ichadon died trying to build a temple for me, I will try to appease his soul by completing it."

The aristocrats had no choice but to agree to the building of a Buddhist temple in Cheongyeongnim. The king had reached a compromise with the nobility and Buddhism was now officially recognized in Silla. All this was thanks to the sacrifice of Ichadon, of course.

Buddhism in the Three Kingdoms period

So, was Ichadon a martyr who gave his life for the sake of Buddhism? It strikes me that he was more of a loyal official

Replica of Mireuksa Temple
Mireuksa originally had one enormous wooden pagoda, flanked by a smaller stone version on each side. Today, all that remains is about half of one stone pagoda in a state of advanced disrepair.

who recognized Beopheung's intention to reinforce his royal authority through the new faith and gave his life for the sake of the king.

The death of Ichadon was the result of a struggle between the king, who wanted to use Buddhism to enhance his royal authority, and aristocrats who wanted to stop the monarch's bid for more power.

Beopheung was not the only king to build large Buddhist temples, stupas and Buddha statues in order to reinforce his own authority. Several other monarchs used the same strategy; prime examples are King Mu of Baekje and King Jinheung of Silla, who built Mireuksa and Hwangnyongsa temples, respectively.

Needed as it was by royal households, Buddhism enjoyed their protection and spread rapidly. This close relationship to royalty is one of the characteristics of Buddhism in the Three Kingdoms period.

A 'sansingak' shrine
Though Buddhism did not originally involve the worship of *sansin* (mountain gods), it came to recognize such deities in Korea after encountering local beliefs. That's why Korean Buddhist temples have *sansingak* and *chilseonggak* shrines.

Hwangnyongsa Temple Site
Hwangnyongsa was the largest temple in Silla. A dragon-emperor appeared when King Jinheung was having a new palace built, prompting the decision to build a temple instead. Later, during the reign of Queen Seondeok, a nine-storey pagoda was erected to demonstrate Silla's all-conquering might to neighboring countries. The tower was burned to the ground by an invading Mongol army during the Goryeo period, however.

Another salient aspect of Buddhism at this time is the way it achieved harmony with ancient local beliefs. You may have noticed that Korean Buddhist temple compounds include a shrine known as the *sansingak*, dedicated to the local mountain god, behind the *daeungjeon* (main shrine hall). Every Buddhist temple in Korea has a *sansingak*, sometimes known as a *chilseonggak* (shrine dedicated to indigenous Korean deity Chilseong) behind or next to its *daeungjeon*. Mountain spirits and Chilseong were not originally worshipped as part of Buddhism. So why do Korean Buddhist temples have *sansingak* and *chilseonggak*?

These shrines appeared as Buddhism moved toward achieving harmony with local beliefs after arriving in Korea. Their worship is an age-old practice passed down through the generations along with the worship of Heaven. Just as a Buddhist temple was built at Cheongyeongnim, a forest used for holding indigenous rites in honor of heaven, *sansingak* shrines and Buddhist temples coexisted side by side.

The *jecheon haengsa* from the Samhan, moreover, was absorbed into the Buddhist "Palgwanhoe" rite. Monks, in place of *mudang*, began praying for blessings and curing illnesses. "*Jung*", one of the Korean words for "Buddhist monk," is said to be derived from the word "*chachaung*." You'll remember how I mentioned the other day that *chachaung* means "*mudang*." All of these phenomena occurred as Buddhism, the new faith, achieved harmony with old beliefs.

Baekje Buddhist culture reaches Japan

In the Japanese city of Nara, near Osaka, is Horyuji Temple, home to one of the oldest wooden buildings in the world. Horyuji was built by Japanese prince Shotoku in order to pray for the repose of his deceased father. Its builders, however, were craftmen from Baekje, Goguryeo and Silla.

Most of the Buddha statues and other items at Horyuji, too, were made by Baekje craftmen.

Of the Three Kingdoms, Baekje had the closest relationship to Japan. The two lands traded actively with each other. At this time, Japan was not the large, powerful country that we know today. Rather, the entity that traded with Baekje was a state known as Wa, located

Gilt-bronze Pensive Maitreya Bodhisattva from the Three Kingdoms period (left) and wooden Pensive Maitreya Bodhisattva from Koryuji Temple in Japan (right) The slightly open eyes, gentle smile and hand held close to the face make these two statues appear like twins. But red pine, the wood from which the Japanese statue is carved, does not grow in Japan. This statue, too, is therefore presumed to have been taken to Japan from Korea.

National Museum of Korea

Jeonju National Museum

Baekje (above) and Japanese (below) gilt-bronze shoes
These two pairs of shoes are highly similar in terms of both form and size. The pair above is from a Baekje tomb in Ipjeom-ri, Iksan, Jeollabuk-do Province, while the pair below is from Eta Funayama tomb in Kumamoto Prefecture, Kyushu, Japan. They measure 31.5 and 29.7 centimeters in length, respectively.

in Nara, a city near Osaka. Its capital was Asuka.

At this time, Wa was ruled by Prince Shotoku. The prince's reign saw great advances in Wa culture, which we now know as "Asuka culture." Its defining characteristic is Buddhism, which came from Baekje.

In the mid-sixth century, King Seong of Baekje sent the monk Norisachigye to Japan with Buddhist images and sutras. Sixteen more monks, including Dosim and Damhye, then crossed the sea to Japan.

Baekje sent not only Buddhism but craftmen specialized in several fields to Japan, to pass on their skills. A succession of specialist Buddha statue makers, temple builders, craftsmen and tile manufacturers travelled from Baekje to Japan.

Buddhist culture transmitted from Baekje was hugely influential in producing Asuka culture.

Baekje also passed on Confucianism and Chinese characters to Japan. Scholars Ajikgi and Wangin introduced the *Analects of Confucius* and the *Thousand Character Classic*, while *ogyeong baksa* such as Danyangi and Goanmu and various experts in fields such as medicine, study of the *I Ching*, astronomy, geography and divination also travelled to Japan.

There's no reason for Koreans to get too big-headed about

the fact that Baekje passed on culture to Japan, or regard Japanese culture today as made by Koreans, however. After all, Korea received a lot of its culture, including Buddhism, from China. Culture is not something that stays in one place; it is constantly changing, influencing other cultures and being influenced by them in turn.

Just as Korea developed its own culture after receiving some from China, Japan has since acquired culture of its own. While it's obvious that Korea passed on culture to Japan in the past, this is not something for Koreans to get conceited about.

Tomb murals with ladies from Susan-ri Goguryeo Tomb (left) and Takamatsuzuka Tomb in Japan (above)
The murals painted in Takamatsuzuka Tomb bear many similarities to those of Goguryeo tombs. Spot the similarities here for yourself.

Influence of the Buddhist culture
of the Three Kingdoms on Asuka

Asuka culture flourished based on Buddhist culture transmitted from
Baekje. Goguryeo and Silla also sent monks, scholars, artists and
craftmen bearing other forms of culture to Japan. The Goguryeo monk
Damjing introduced techniques for making paint, ink and paper, while
the monk Hyeja tutored Prince Shotoku. Many items of cultural heritage
that survive in Japan today were influenced by the culture of the Three
Kingdoms.

Baekje Avalokitesvara
statue, Horyuji Temple
This statue of the
Bodhisattva Avalokitesvara
is housed at Horyuji
Temple in Japan. Standing
over two meters tall, it has
a beautifully elegant poise.

Five-storey wooden
pagoda at Horyuji Temple
This pagoda demonstrates
the transmission of Baekje
pagoda building techniques
to Japan.

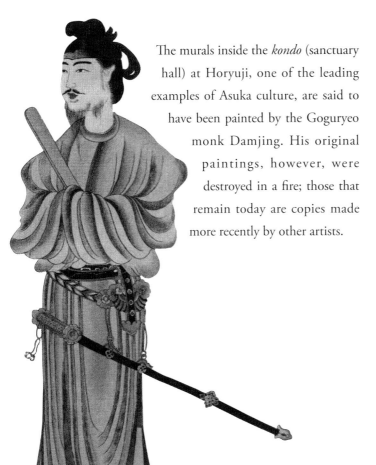

The murals inside the *kondo* (sanctuary hall) at Horyuji, one of the leading examples of Asuka culture, are said to have been painted by the Goguryeo monk Damjing. His original paintings, however, were destroyed in a fire; those that remain today are copies made more recently by other artists.

Kondo (sanctuary hall) mural
This is a restored version of a mural said to have been painted by Damjing, a Goguryeo monk who had travelled to Japan.

Portrait of Prince Shotoku by Crown Prince Ajwa of Baekje
Crown Prince Ajwa, son of Wideok, the twenty-seventh king of Baekje, was an excellent artist. Ajwa traveled to Japan, where he is said to have painted this portrait of Prince Shotoku. The original version, housed at Horyuji Temple, was destroyed in a fire, so that this reproduction is all that remains.

CHAPTER 10

Life in the Three Kingdoms period

Did they have dining tables in those days? Murals in two Goguryeo tombs, Muyongchong and Gakjeochong, clearly portray people sitting and eating with tables in front of them. We have to remember, however, that the people depicted in these murals are not commoners but of high social status. Dining tables were not used by everyone. Ordinary people probably just ate from dishes placed straight on the floor.

TIME LINE -------- 427 -------- 475 -------- 527 --------

Goguryeo
Capital moved to
Pyeongyang

Baekje
Capital moved
to Ungjin

Silla
Ichadon put to death;
Buddhism officially
recognized

Some of the main sources of information available to us when it comes to what the people of the Three Kingdoms looked like, what clothes they wore and how they lived are tomb murals. Other sources, such as figures made from earthenware or clay, also offer clues about life in those days.

To look at a Goguryeo tomb mural is like watching a scene from a film. The people in them are portrayed so vividly that they could come to life at any moment. The mural below shows a Goguryeo nobleman receiving guests. He is entertaining them in a huge room festooned with beautiful drapes. Of the three men sitting down, the one on the right is the host; the two opposite him are his guests. The servant attending to them is depicted as a very small figure. One of the guests is busily telling the others a story, illustrated with hand gestures. In front of each guest and the host is a full dining table, while the tables behind them are piled with still more food.

Today, let's look a little closer at how people in the Three Kingdoms period actually lived.

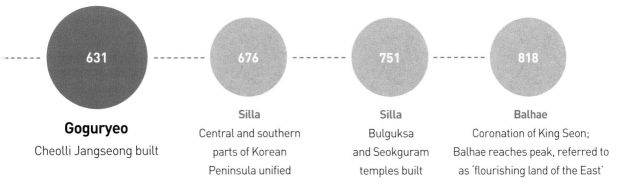

631	676	751	818
Goguryeo	Silla	Silla	Balhae
Cheolli Jangseong built	Central and southern parts of Korean Peninsula unified	Bulguksa and Seokguram temples built	Coronation of King Seon; Balhae reaches peak, referred to as 'flourishing land of the East'

What did people eat during the Three Kingdoms period? Did they have meat, like us?

Meat was not easily available to everyone. To all but the king and the aristocracy, it was a rare treat. People in the Three Kingdoms ate pork, chicken, venison and pheasant. Cows came to Korea later than other animals and were not eaten but used as working beasts on farms.

When eating meat, people at this time liked to grill it on the spot at braziers placed next to the dining table. So it seems that Korea's fondness for grilling meat like *bulgogi* (marinated beef) or *galbi* (ribs) at their dining tables today is a tradition with roots deep in the past.

Goguryeo gods of fire and agriculture
These murals are located in a Goguryeo tomb in Ji'an, in China's Jilin Province. On the left is the god of fire; on the right, the god of agriculture. The former carries flames, while the latter, who has the head of a cow, carries ears of rice.

A Goguryeo kitchen
This mural from Tomb No. 3 at Anak in Hwanghae-do Province shows people at work in a kitchen. One is busy preparing food in front of a steamer, while another is lighting a fire in the fireplace. Another person is clearing dishes. The meat safe is full of hanging carcasses. It's more than likely that this was the kitchen of an aristocrat's house.

Rice: the food of kings and noblemen

Pure white rice, another food universally available today, was also hard to come by for most people in the Three Kingdoms period. Only kings and aristocrats were able to eat it; everyone else had to mix small amounts of valuable rice with barley, soy beans or millet.

Methods of cooking rice also changed. At first, it was cooked in a steamer, but later in the Three Kingdoms period it was placed in a covered pot - which, according to scholars, was when our own method of cooking rice originated.

Did people eat three meals a day, like we do? No, in those days they normally ate just twice: once in the morning and once in the evening. Even King Taejong Muyeol of Silla, renowned as a big eater, normally skipped lunch. He only ate three meals a day during the fight to conquer Baekje, for extra strength.

What kind of side dishes did they eat? Kimchi. You'll recall how I mentioned that the kimchi eaten back then was not red or spicy but made by pickling radish in salt. Other side dishes included fermented soy bean paste and pickled fish. The people of Goguryeo were renowned, even in China, for their skill in making fermented food.

On a normal day, then, most people ate cooked barley, millet or soy beans with soup or stew made from bean paste or salt and pickled radish as a side dish. They ate meat only once or twice a year, on special occasions.

Kings and noblemen, of course, ate splendid meals. King Taejong Muyeol ate three *mal* (a traditional unit of capacity) of rice and nine pheasants and drank six *mal* of wine every day, while Prince Chadeuk, younger brother of King Munmu, had fifty different dishes served when entertaining guests. Ordinary people, however, could never even have dreamt of eating like that.

Did they have dining tables in those days? Murals in two Goguryeo tombs, Muyongchong and Gakjeochong, clearly

Silla steamers and earthenware stove
These artifacts were discovered at Naengsu-ri in Pohang. The steamers are very similar to those we use today.
–Gyeongju National Museum

Goguryeo aristocrats at dinner
This scene from a mural at Muyongchong Tomb shows aristocrats sitting before dining tables.

portray people sitting and eating with tables in front of them. We have to remember, however, that the people depicted in these murals are not commoners but of high social status. Dining tables were not used by everyone. Ordinary people probably just ate from dishes placed straight on the floor.

A house for every status

House-shaped earthenware vessel
Would everyday commoners have lived in houses like this one?
– Gyeongju National Museum

What were homes like in the Three Kingdoms period? Advances in heating technology meant there was no longer any need to dig down into the ground like before. Houses were built entirely above the ground, like those we live in today. Heating was provided by stones laid out in an L shape on one side of the room. Once heated by fire, these kept the room nice and warm. This system, known as *jjokgudeul*, was a precursor to *ondol*, which heats the entire floor of a room but had not been invented at the time.

Since the *jjokgudeul* system only heated part of the floor, people avoided direct contact with it by using beds and chairs.

House-shaped Silla cinerary urn
This vessel was used to contain the ashes of those cremated in accordance with Buddhist tradition. The straight lines of its tiled roof are reminiscent of a Silla aristocrat's home.
– Gyeongju National Museum

Ordinary people lived in homes with thatched roofs, but the ruling classes built houses with tiled roofs and decorated their rooms with beautiful drapes, beds and chairs.

Seohyeon and Manmyeong in love

How did men and women meet each other in the Three Kingdoms period? If you thought relationships before marriage were forbidden, and that people got married to partners chosen by their parents without so much as catching a glimpse of each other's face before the wedding, you're wrong.

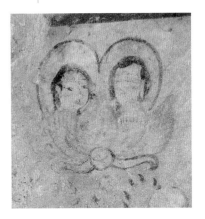

Rebirth in a lotus flower
This beautiful image of a man and woman in a lotus flower is part of a mural in Tomb No. 1 in Changchuan, Manchuria. It expresses the hope that the couple buried here will be reborn together in the next world and enjoy a good relationship there.

Let me tell you the story of Seohyeon and Manmyeong, two lovers that lived in Silla 1,400 years ago. The way they dated freely and their bold love appears no different to young people today.

Kim Seohyeon belonged to a royal family in Gaya. If his country had not fallen, he may even have become king one day. When Gaya eventually submitted to Silla, however, its royal families became Silla citizens.

Walking down the road one day, Seohyeon caught sight of a girl whose beauty moved his heart. Her name was Manmyeong and she was the daughter of Sukheuljong, younger brother of King Jinheung of Silla, making her a very high-born young lady indeed. It appears that Manmyeong

Clay figurines of a Silla couple
The poses and expressions of these two clay figurines are so lifelike, it seems they will spring into action at any moment.
– Gyeongju National Museum

quite liked the look Seohyeon, too. They fell in love.

A while later, Seohyeon was appointed governor-general of Manno-gun (today's Jincheon in Chuncheongbuk-do Province) and set out on the long journey to his new post. He wanted, of course, to take Manmyeong with him. Manmyeong's father, who only now realized that his daughter was Seohyeon's lover, had her locked up in another part of the palace and posted a guard to keep an eye on her.

Suddenly, an almighty bolt of lightning struck. While her stunned guard was still trying to gather his wits, Manmyeong escaped and ran off to Manno-gun with Seohyeon. Later, the couple had a handsome son who grew up to become one of Silla's most famous generals, Kim Yusin. This story appears in the biography of Kim Yusin contained in *Samguk sagi*.

Silla society did not forbid men and women from mingling. The same went for Goguryeo and Baekje. Ancient Chinese history books describe how Goguryeo "people love singing and dancing. When the sun goes down, men and women come together and enjoy singing to one another" and how "men and women get married because they love each other."

In other words, many couples got married because they wanted just like Seohyeon and Manmyeong, although the normal thing would still have been for parents to arrange their children's marriages.

Picture of a couple from Ssangyeongchong Tomb
The husband and wife laid to rest in this tomb are sitting on a wooden bench with their shoes off. Beside them is a very small picture of a servant attending to them. Ssangyeongchong Tomb in Yonggang, Nampo, Pyeongannam-do Province. Ssangyeongchong, which means "twin columns tomb," is named for the two octagonal columns inside it.

A woman in the Three Kingdoms Period
This image is part of a mural in Tomb No. 3 at Anak in Hwanghae-do Province. Married women wore their hair up in arrangements like this.

Moving in with the bride's family

What were weddings like in the Three Kingdoms period? *Dongyizhuan* in the Chinese history *Sanguozhi* contains a description of a Goguryeo wedding.

In Goguryeo, once a promise of marriage had been made, the bride's family would build another house behind the family home. This was known as a *seook*, meaning "son-in-law's house." On the wedding night, the groom would stand before the bride's house, state his name, go down onto his knees and bow, then ask several times to be let in. If the bride's parents granted him permission, he would enter the *seook*... Only when a baby was born to the new couple and it had grown up would they move back to the groom's home.

Couples would get married at the bride's house, carry on living there after the wedding, and eventually return to the groom's home once their children had grown up. This custom existed not only in Goguryeo but also in Silla and Baekje. It continued all the way through the subsequent Goryeo period, too, and into early Joseon. Only in late Joseon did the custom change, so that now a newlywed bride went to live with the groom's family.

What kind of wedding gifts did families exchange? In Goguryeo, the groom's family sent pork and wine to that of the bride; no jewellery was exchanged. If a bride's family had accepted jewellery from that of the groom, others would have criticized them for selling their daughter as a slave. In Silla, too, only wine and food were prepared for wedding ceremonies. A bride's family never gave their new in-laws wedding gifts or a dowry.

Doesn't that seem much better than nowadays, when brides and grooms get so stressed about wedding gifts that they sometimes end up calling off the wedding altogether? It seems love and marriage in the Three Kingdoms period, in their own way, were more sophisticated than today.

Social status systems
Such systems existed not only in the Three Kingdoms period but also in Goryeo and Joseon. In fact, they were not confined to Korea but existed in almost every country in the world. Whether a society has a status system or not can be taken as a measure of how far it has developed. Nowadays, such systems have disappeared from almost all countries.

Status determined by birth

A social status system classifies people into strata according to criteria such as lineage, family, property or power. Social status in the Three Kingdoms was inherited from birth and could not be changed at will.

How would you like it if you were forced to settle for your given status, regardless of your own ability? If you were born a slave and condemned to remain so all your life, no matter how clever and wise you were, you would find it very unfair. At the time of the Three Kingdoms, however, it didn't even cross people's minds that such predetermined social status was unfair. They accepted it as something natural.

The people of the Three Kingdoms were divided into three social categories: aristocrats, commoners and slaves. Highest up in the aristocracy, of course, was the king. Social status determined the clothing people wore, the food they ate, the houses they lived in, the work they did and the positions they held.

Goguryeo tomb murals depict people in different sizes according to their social statuses. Noblemen are large, while the servants attending to them are very small. Even pictures reflected social status.

The aristocracy made up the ruling

Aristocrat and slave
This is a scene from a mural at Muyongchong, a Goguryeo tomb. Murals such as this one demonstrated differences in social status by depicting aristocrats in large forms and slaves half their size.

• Caste systems in the Three Kingdoms

King and queen
Though kings were at the very top of
the social order, they were sometimes
outmaneuvered by aristocrats. This is
why they were always looking for ways to
enhance royal authority.

Commoners
Commoners spent most
of their time farming, but
were forced to go and work
as laborers for no pay
whenever the state built a
fortress or castle.

Aristocracy
Aristocrats owned land and slaves and held
government positions, thereby dominating
politics and society.

classes that controlled society. They possessed government positions, land and slaves and enjoyed many privileges. Most commoners were farmers, forced to pay taxes to the state.

There were three forms of tax: paying grain or produce such as rice, soy beans or millet; paying in fabric like hemp or silk; and providing unpaid labour on building sites for fortresses or palaces, or joining the army. Neither aristocrats nor slaves paid taxes: this burden lay entirely with commoners.

Slaves, holders of the lowest social status, were treated as assets or possessions of their masters, for whom they farmed or did housework.

Could the people of Goguryeo, Baekje and Silla understand each other?

Did people in Goguryeo and Baekje speak the same language? Some claim that the two states would have shared a language since Baekje had branched off from Goguryeo, while others assert that Baekje's ruling class spoke the same language as Goguryeo but its commoners spoke something else. So who's right? I think that, even if the ruling classes and commoners spoke different languages at first, the passing of time would have eliminated any communication problems.

What were the languages of Goguryeo and Silla like, then? According to scholars who have studied the way Goguryeo place names are written in *Samguk sagi*, the languages of Silla and Goguryeo were either similar or the same. Which means that people from each of the Three Kingdoms could have spoken to each other without interpreters.

Fridges and drinks

At a time when nobody had fridges or freezers, ice was a highly important and valuable commodity. States put a lot of care into managing their ice reserves. They would carve hard blocks of ice in winter, put them in specially made ice storehouses and use them in summer.

Seokbinggo, Gyeongju
A *seokbinggo* was like a Three Kingdoms version of a fridge. Ice was cut in winter, stored in the *seokbinggo* and taken out for use in summer. Since ice was a very valuable commodity in summer, it was managed by the state and used by the royal household or distributed to officials. Getting hold of ice would not have been easy for commoners. The *seokbinggo* in this photo was rebuilt in the Joseon period.

Seokbinggo, a structure in today's Gyeongju, is an ice storehouse built of stone. Silla began storing ice for future use during the reign of King Jijeung, while the practice began in Goguryeo under King Yuri.

The proper storage and distribution of ice reserves as and when needed were very important national events. Silla created a government office called the Binggojeon and entrusted it with all ice-related matters. A rite was performed every time the door of an ice storehouse was opened. Such practices continued into the Goryeo and Joseon periods.

We now think of milk as a Western import, but in fact our ancestors began drinking it long ago.

A Japanese book called *Shinsen shojiroku* ("Newly Selected Records of Family Names and Titles") relates how Boksang, a Baekje man, travelled to Japan in the mid-seventh century and taught the locals how to milk cows.

Today's milk is available to anyone, young or old, but in those days it was a very precious liquid drunk only by kings and nobles. It remained this way through the Goryeo period, when a government office in charge of cow milking, called the Yuuso, was established.

What else did people drink? The biography of Kim Yusin in *Samguk sagi* contains a passage that relates how Kim, having returned from one battle, passed right by his own front door without seeing his family and carried on toward the next battlefield. Kim suddenly stopped his horse and gave an order to one of his subordinates:

Jaemaejeong Well
The well to the right of this monument house is located at the site where Kim Yusin's house once stood. It is six meters deep. The well is called Jaemaejeong; Kim Yusin's house was later named after it. It is located in Gyo-dong, Gyeongju.

"Bring me some *jangsu* from my house."

Kim gulped downed the cup of *jangsu* and spoke happily;

"Tastes just the same as it always did."

What was the "*jangsu*" that Kim drank? It seems likely to have been a drink made from fermented rice, but it no longer exists today so we can't be sure. The people of Silla also dried peppermint leaves and used them to make tea.

CHAPTER 11

How did Silla achieve unification?

Baekje and Goguryeo eventually fell to an alliance formed by Silla and Tang.

What do you think of Kim Chunchu's diplomacy? Wasn't it a terrible thing to join forces with Tang, another country altogether, to bring down two fellow Korean states? At that time, you know, the peoples of the Three Kingdoms didn't think of themselves as belonging to the same nation. The very concept of a nation was alien to them.

TIME LINE

427
Goguryeo
Capital moved to
Pyeongyang

475
Baekje
Capital moved
to Ungjin

527
Silla
Ichadon put to death;
Buddhism officially
recognized

What's the first thing you think of when someone mentions the unification of the Korean Peninsula by Silla?

People like General Kim Yusin, Gwanchang the Hwarang and General Gyebaek?

Or have you ever wished that Goguryeo, not Silla had unified the Three Kingdoms?

Silla was the latest developer among the three states. So how did it bring down Baekje and Goguryeo? By getting help from Tang? Or thanks to some unique strength of its own? In fact, did Silla really unify the Three Kingdoms at all?

Silla's unification of Korea raises a lot of questions. Today, I'll try and answer a few of them.

First of all, though, let's look at the last days of Baekje and Goguryeo. If we understand what brought these two states to their ends, it'll be easier to understand how Silla achieved unification.

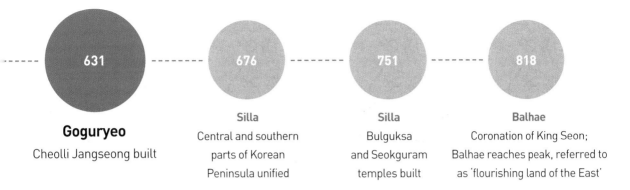

631	676	751	818

Goguryeo
Cheolli Jangseong built

Silla
Central and southern
parts of Korean
Peninsula unified

Silla
Bulguksa
and Seokguram
temples built

Balhae
Coronation of King Seon;
Balhae reaches peak, referred to
as 'flourishing land of the East'

In Nonsan, Chungcheongnam-do Province is a place that was once called "Hwangsanbeol." These days, it's a peaceful field of golden rice plants, but around 1,350 years ago it was the site of the last battle between Silla and Baekje. Silla's army was commanded by Kim Yusin and Baekje's by Gyebaek - the top generals in their respective countries.

Chungjangsa
Located in Nonsan,
Chungcheongnam-do,
where the Battle of
Hwangsanbeol was fought,
this shrine is dedicated to
General Gyebaek. Near it
are a tomb thought to be
that of Gyebaek and Baekje
Military Museum.

Baekje's last stand at Hwangsanbeol

In 660, Silla joined forces with Tang and attacked Baekje. Their aim was to take the latter's capital, Sabiseong Fortress. You will recall that Sabiseong was located in what is

Busosanseong Mountain Fortress, Buyeo
This fortress surrounds Mt. Busosan, the former site of a Baekje royal palace. It is also sometimes known as Sabiseong or Soburiseong. It was normally a back garden for the palace, but seems to have been used defensively in times of war. Within the fortress are Nakhwaam Rock, famous for the story of the 3,000 court ladies, and Goransa Temple.

now the town of Buyeo. Tang's forces sailed across the Yellow Sea and landed on the banks of the Geumgang River, while Silla made its way overland via Tanhyeon.

Leading a desperate band of 5,000 men, General Gyebaek of Baekje set out to stop the Silla army. The latter had some 50,000 men - ten times more than Baekje. Before he left for the battlefield, Gyebaek summoned his wife and children and bade them farewell.

"If you were taken prisoner you'd become slaves of the enemy. Better to die than live such a life."

Gyebaek raised his sword and cut down his beloved family. He knew he would not be coming back alive, and that there was no way Baekje could win the battle.

The general struck camp at a high vantage point and waited for the Silla army to arrive. The invading forces wavered when they came before the Baekje army of men prepared to fight to the death. General Kim Heumsun of Silla, realizing that something needed to be done, summoned his son, Bangul, and sent him to the enemy camp for a duel. After fighting bravely, he was killed.

Next, General Kim Pumil sent his son, Gwanchang, to fight. The young man jumped up onto his horse and galloped over to the Baekje camp, alone. He, too, fought bravely but was captured.

When Gyebaek took off Gwanchang's helmet, he found a baby-faced youth. Unable to bring himself to kill the boy, he set him free. But Gwanchang once again took up his spear and charged at the enemy camp. Finally, Gyebaek cut his head off, tied him to his horse's saddle and sent him back to the Silla army.

Enraged by the deaths of Bangul and Gwanchang, the Silla forces wasted no more time in launching an all-out attack. This is exactly what Kim Heumsun and Kim Pumil had hoped

The Battle of Hwangsanbeol
The battle between a desperate band of 5,000 Baekje men and a Silla army of 50,000 at Hwangsanbeol was a decisive moment in the fate of Baekje.

Baengmagang River seen from Nakhwaam Rock
The back of Busosanseong Mountain Fortress is a sheer cliff, below which flows the Baengmagang River. How must those court ladies have felt as they threw themselves off the cliff to avoid falling into the hands of the enemy?

to achieve by sending their sons to the enemy camp. Bangul and Gwanchang were sacrificed for the sake of Silla.

Each of Baekje's men fought his utmost, but the defenders were simply overwhelmed. The tide of battle reversed over and over again, but eventually Gyebaek and all his men were killed. Their blood stained the ground at Hwangsanbeol red.

After beating Gyebaek's band of resistance fighters, the Silla army swept effortlessly on to Sabiseong. Tang forces poured in at the same time. Eventually, the Baekje capital fell. King Uija had already fled to Ungjinseong Fortress, but all those who had not yet managed to escape were killed or taken prisoner. This is when the sad story of the 3,000 court ladies at Nakhwaam Rock took place. Nakhwaam, meaning "rock of falling flowers," gets its name from an episode in which 3,000 Baekje court ladies, fleeing enemy forces, jumped off the rock into the river far below, falling through the air like flower petals in the wind. We can't know for sure if there were actually 3,000 ladies, but it was certainly a large number.

The allied Silla and Tang forces also took Ungjinseong, to which King Uija had fled. Uija and crown prince Hyo poured wine for Tang general Su Dingfang as an expression of surrender.

King Uija and some 12,000 Baekje retainers and commoners were taken away to Tang, where Uija grew ill and died. And that's how 700 years of Baekje history came to an end.

Yeon Gaesomun's sons fight among themselves

Tang's real target was Goguryeo. It had joined forces with Silla because it wanted to get the latter out of Baekje before conquering Goguryeo.

The year after it had taken Sabiseong, Tang sent its forces up the Daedonggang River and laid siege to the Goguryeo capital, Pyeongyangseong Fortress. This was the first time Pyeongyangseong had ever come under siege, but it didn't fall as easily as Sabiseong. Goguryeo proved amazingly strong. In the end, the Tang army had no choice but to retreat.

Only a few years later, though, Goguryeo was gone. How could this have happened? The main reasons were a power struggle in its ruling class, and internal divisions. After Yeon Gaesomun died, his sons began fighting among themselves for power.

Yeon Gaesomun held power for twenty-four years. There was a king, but only by name: Yeon was in charge of actual politics. When he fell ill and died, all the discontent that had been building up finally erupted. His three sons, Namsaeng, Namgeon and Namsan, began a struggle to become the most powerful man in Goguryeo.

As he lay dying, Yeon Gaesomun left his sons with some last words:

"You three must stay in harmony, like fish and water. Under no circumstances must you fight."

Pyeongyangseong Fortress's last stand Goguryeo, having brushed off the mighty armies of Sui Emperor Yangdi and Tang Emperor Taizong, eventually fell because of a power struggle among its ruling classes - I guess that shows how dangerous such internal rifts can be.

His sons, however, failed to follow his wishes. When the eldest, Namsaeng took a trip outside the capital, second son Namgeon opportunistically took over his position. When Namsaeng, heard about this, he sent his own son, Heonseong, to Tang to plead for help in conquering Goguryeo. Tang, which had been eyeing up Goguryeo, jumped at the chance and immediately launched an invasion with Heonseong as its guide.

Battering ram
This weapon was used for crashing hard into fortress gates and walls and destroying them.

High ladder
This tall ladder was used for attacking fortresses. The ladder is unfolded, placed against the fortress wall, and climbed.
–The War Memorial of Korea

In January, 668 Tang troops descended upon Pyeongyangseong. A Silla army also advanced on the Goguryeo capital at Tang's request and the allied armies surrounded it. Namsaeng now came up with a crafty trick: he sent a spy to Sinseong, one of Namgeon's retainers, saying he would give him a big reward if he opened the city gates.

"I'll look for a chance to open them" Sinseong replied.

Sure enough, five days later, the gates opened. Some 500 mounted Silla troops spearheaded the attack, followed by Tang forces. The allied armies went on the rampage, burning down palaces and houses. They say Pyeongyangseong went on burning for four months, so you can imagine the extent of the destruction.

What became of Namsaeng and his son Heonseong, who had guided the Tang forces to Pyeongyangseong? They were rewarded by Tang with government positions. Later, though, Heonseong was charged with trying to start a rebellion and executed. Namgeon was taken to Tang as a prisoner. So were Goguryeo King Bojang, his sons and around 200,000 other people.

After conquering Baekje and Goguryeo, Tang granted Silla no power whatsoever. It established outposts called "Andong Duhufu" ("Protectorate-General to Pacify the East") at Pyeongyangseong and *"Xiongjin Dudufu"* ("Ungjin

Daedongmun Gate, Pyeongyangseong Fortress
Pyeongyangseong's eastern gate, Daedongmun, was its most important entrance. The Daedongmun that remains today is a reconstruction dating from the Joseon period. This picture was painted by British artist Elizabeth Keith on a visit to Korea in 1919.

Commandery") at Sabiseong to rule the former territories of Goguryeo and Baekje, respectively.

Silla therefore decided it was time for a fight with Tang. Its forces inflicted heavy defeats on Chinese armies at Maesoseong Fortress in what is now Yangju in Gyeonggi-do Province, and at Gibeolpo at the mouth of the Geumgang River. Tang, judging that any further fighting would be to its disadvantage, moved the Protectorate-General to Pacify the East and Ungjin Commandery to Manchuria. Silla was now in control of the Korean Peninsula all the way up to a line that stretched roughly from the Daedonggang River to the Bay of Wonsan. In other words, it had unified the central and southern parts of Korea.

Stone fragment of Pyeongyangseong Fortress with inscription
This stone contains an inscription recording the building site zones and individuals responsible for them when Pyeongyangseong was built. It reads: "Construction began on May 28 in the Year Gichuk [569]. The segment running west for eleven *ri* was overseen by Sangbu Yak Mori, an official of *sohyeong* rank."

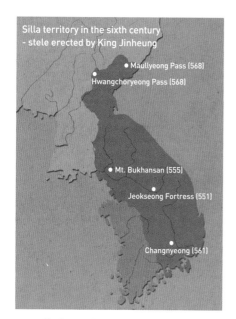

Silla territory in the sixth century
- stele erected by King Jinheung

● Maullyeong Pass (568)
● Hwangchoryeong Pass (568)

● Mt. Bukhansan (555)
● Jeokseong Fortress (551)

● Changnyeong (561)

Having previously been the least developed of the Three Kingdoms, Silla began advancing around the beginning of the sixth century.

King Jinheung Sunsubi Monument, Mt. Bukhansan
After Silla had taken control of the Hangang region, King Jinheung erected a memorial stone at the top of Mt. Bukhansan. This is what we now call the King Jinheung Sunsubi Monument. It is housed in the National Museum of Korea.

The Hangang River:
Silla's stepping stone to unification

Silla developed latest among the Three Kingdoms. So how did it end up achieving unification?

Silla's retaking of the Hangang River region served as a stepping stone on its way to supremacy. As I mentioned before, this area is at the center of the Korean Peninsula and can be reached directly from China by boat. This is why the Three Kingdoms competed so fiercely to gain control of it.

Silla captured the Hangang region during the reign of King Jinheung. At the time, the area was controlled by Goguryeo. Jinheung and King Seong of Baekje put together an allied army to attack their northern neighbor; by now the two southern kingdoms had been partners for more than 100 years. You will remember that this was known as the "Naje Alliance."

Silla and Baekje pulled off a nicely executed maneuver and captured the Hangang region. They then divided it amicably between themselves, with Silla in possession of the upper reaches of the river and Baekje the lower reaches. Two years later, however, King Jinheung suddenly attacked Baekje's territory around the lower part of the Hangang. Caught by surprise,

Samnyeonsanseong Mountain Fortress
Located in Boeun, Chungcheongbuk-do Province, this fortress was used by Silla as a base for attacking Baekje. The hard fighting by Silla forces stationed here in the battle at Gwansanseong led to the death of King Seong of Baekje. The fortress is so-named because it took three years to build.

Baekje was defeated and Silla gained control of the entire river. The alliance between the two states, which had lasted for over a century, was broken overnight by Silla's treachery.

A furious King Seong of Baekje now invaded Silla. The two states clashed at Gwansanseong Mountain Fortress, in what is now Okcheon, Chungcheonbuk-do Province. At first, Baekje had the upper hand, but reinforcements from Silla arrived in the nick of time. Their commander was Kim Muryeok, grandfather of Kim Yusin. As soon as the extra men arrived, the newly emboldened Silla troops won a crushing victory. It was here that King Seong of Baekje died, in battle.

By winning the battle at Gwansanseong, Silla escaped its third-place status among the Three Kingdoms, paving the way for development. As well as expanding its territory, it now began direct exchange with China. The southeastern state had taken the lead in the tight contest between the Three Kingdoms. What do you think of Jinheung's choice to break the Naje alliance that had been in place for so long and attack Baekje? Was he a hero who expanded his country's territory and laid the foundations for unification, or a traitor who broke his promise? Isn't it all right to break a promise for the sake of your country? Think about it.

Kim Chunchu: Korean traitor?

Once Silla had taken control of the Hangang region, Baekje began a series of persistent attacks on its eastern neighbor. Because of Silla, Baekje had lost both a valuable piece of territory and its own king - we can only imagine how incensed it must have been.

Harassed by Baekje's attacks, Silla sent an envoy to Goguryeo proposing that the two states form an alliance to set upon Baekje. This envoy was Kim Chunchu, great-grandson of King Jinheung. When Kim arrived in Goguryeo, however, Yeon Gaesomun threw him into prison.

After barely managing to escape from Goguryeo, Kim now turned to Tang. There, Emperor Gaozong accepted Kim's proposal to attack Baekje. His intention was to bring down Baekje, then Goguryeo and finally even Silla, thus bringing the entire Korean Peninsula under Tang control. This was how the Silla-Tang alliance I mentioned earlier came to turn on Baekje. It was to this partnership that the southwestern state and Goguryeo eventually fell.

What do you think of Kim Chunchu's diplomacy? Wasn't it a terrible thing to join forces with Tang, another country altogether, to bring down two fellow Korean states? At that time, you know, the peoples of the Three Kingdoms didn't think of themselves as belonging to the same nation. The very concept of a nation was alien to them. So it seems we cannot label Kim Chunchu and the people of Silla at the time traitors for seeking the help of another nation to conquer parts of their own.

Kim Chunchu took the throne, becoming the king we now

King Munmu's dying wish

As he lay dying, King Munmu of Silla, the man who had unified the Korean Peninsula below the line from the Daedonggang to the Bay of Wonsan, left a last wish:

"When I die, let me lie in state for ten days, then cremate me. Hold my funeral on a big rock in the East Sea. I want to become a dragon and protect my country."

In accordance with his wish, Munmu was cremated and his funeral held on the sea off Gampo, on the east coast. Today, you can still find a rocky island off the coast of Gampo, known as Daewangam ("Great King Rock"); it is here that King Munmu's funeral was held.

Daewangam
Towards the center of the island is a turtle-shaped granite boulder; below this is what is known as 'Haejungneung' ("Royal tomb in the Sea"). Some say that this is not a tomb but the site where King Munmu's ashes were scattered after cremation.

know as Taejong Muyeol. He died the year after the fall of Baekje. From the start, his aim had always been to conquer Silla's western neighbor. It never occurred to him to do the same to Goguryeo. It was Taejong Muyeol's son, King Munmu, who unified the Korean Peninsula below the line stretching from the Daedonggang to the Bay of Wonsan. At this time, though, the area unified by Silla contained none of Goguryeo's territory: only that of Silla and Baekje. What became of Goguryeo's former territory, then? At first, its former citizens scattered. Thirty years later, however, in 698, they founded another state called Balhae. Which means Silla didn't unify all Three Kingdoms after all...

So why do people so often go on about Silla unifying the Three Kingdoms, or talk about "Unified Silla?" When did the name Unified Silla come into existence? The people of Silla never used it themselves. Surprisingly, this term was coined for the very first time by Japanese scholars researching Korean history during the colonial period, it in order to justify ruling the country as a Japanese colony. By claiming that Silla unified all three kingdoms, these scholars were sneakily pushing Goguryeo's magnificent past and territory out of Korean history.

?!

Hwarang: boys as beautiful as flowers

Gwanchang, the young man who gave his life for his country in the final battle between Baekje and Silla at Hwangsanbeol, was a "Hwarang." So was the famous general Kim Yusin. In fact, nearly all of Silla's top military commanders came from the ranks of the Hwarang.

The Hwarang were members of a unique group of young men in Silla. Their roots lay in the Wonhwa, a group led by two beautiful women. But these two leaders, Nammo and Junjeong, were jealous of each other. Junjeong got Nammo drunk, then threw her into a river. When the crime was discovered, she, too, was put to death. The Wonhwa thus ended in failure.

King Jinheung changed the Wonhwa into the Hwarang. Unlike the Wonhwa, the Hwarang were led by men. The name Hwarang means "boys as beautiful as flowers." Jinheung created the order to cultivate men of talent and warriors. Not just anyone could become a Hwarang, however - only those of "true-bone" rank (see Chapter 12) and above were eligible. Meanwhile, the ranks of their attendants, known as "*nangdo*," were also open to commoners. Hwarang were aged between fifteen and eighteen years old.

Hwarang lived communally for three years, cultivating their minds and bodies as they learned martial arts and travelled to beautiful places. When war broke out, they fought for their country and were ready to lay down their lives. They were instrumental in Silla's efforts for unification. Later, however, they began devoting more attention to having fun than to self-cultivation.

A Silla Hwarang

CHAPTER 12

Silla,
land of the
bone-rank system

No matter how great their talent, those of six-head rank were never able to escape the shadow of the true-bone rank above them.

This is why many men of six-head rank gave up the pursuit of government positions altogether, becoming monks, scholars, or unofficial royal advisors. Wonhyo, a famous monk of whom you may have heard, was also of six-head rank.

TIME LINE	427	475	527
	Goguryeo Capital moved to Pyeongyang	**Baekje** Capital moved to Ungjin	**Silla** Ichadon put to death; Buddhism officially recognized

In my last letter, I explained how Silla brought down Goguryeo and Baekje and unified the central and southern parts of the Korean Peninsula. Today, let's travel back to post-unification Silla.

After unification, Silla enjoyed around 200 years without war. If the Three Kingdoms period was one of endless conflict. The new one was of peace and stability.

Since before unification, Silla had had a unique caste structure known as the "bone-rank" (golpum) system. This system classified people into one of several bone-ranks or "head-ranks" and was entirely hereditary.

Goguryeo and Baekje also had caste systems of their own, as did Japan, China, India and Europe, as you'll recall. It's hard to find, however, another order that affected every last aspect of people's daily lives as deeply Silla's bone-rank system. If you want to understand life in Silla, therefore, you need to be aware of it.

Let's have a look at how the people of Silla lived according to their bone-rank system.

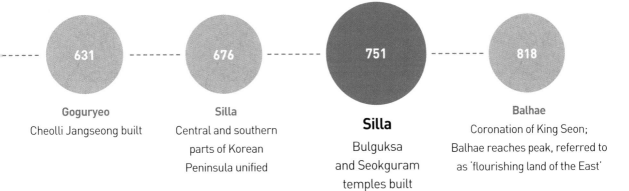

631
Goguryeo
Cheolli Jangseong built

676
Silla
Central and southern
parts of Korean
Peninsula unified

751
Silla
Bulguksa
and Seokguram
temples built

818
Balhae
Coronation of King Seon;
Balhae reaches peak, referred to
as 'flourishing land of the East'

The bone-rank system consisted of two bone-ranks - "sacred-bone" and "true-bone" - and six head-ranks. Below those of head-rank status were commoners. Among the head-ranks, six was the highest and one the lowest. As time passed, however, those of the lower three ranks came to receive the same treatment as commoners. Eventually, then, Silla's bone-rank system consisted of sacred-bone, true-bone, head-rank six to four, and commoners.

The facts of life in Silla

Those of sacred-bone and true-bone status were royalty, eligible to rise to the very highest government positions. Scholars remain divided as to how the sacred-bone and

● **Various Silla roof tiles**
– Gyeongju National Museum

Tile with goblin design

Convex antefix
with face design

Convex antefixes with lotus flower designs

Convex antefix with   Convex antefix with
honeysuckle and 'bosang'   Buddha design
flower design

Concave antefix with
arabesque design

Concave antefix
with 'girin' design

true-bone ranks differed, but the former is thought not to have been part of the original ranking structure and to have appeared some time between the reigns of Beopheung and Jinheung or Jinpyeong, as part of a process of royal authority.

Social status placed limits on how high a government position an individual could hold. Those of true-bone rank were eligible to become *ibeolchan*, the highest-ranking position, but those of head-rank six could only rise as far as *achan*, the sixth-highest post; those of head-rank five only as far as *daenama*, the tenth-highest; and those of head-rank four only as far as *daesa*, the twelfth-highest.

Even the most talented individuals were unable to break through the hereditary bone ceiling imposed by the system, which permeated every aspect of daily life. Marriage, too, took place between those of the same bone-rank. The clothes people wore, the sizes of their houses and even the dishes from which they ate every day were all determined in detail by bone-rank regulations.

The colors and materials of women's outer skirts, inner skirts, hairpins and combs were all regulated. The

A Silla aristocratic household
In Silla, everything from the size of homes to the
type of dishes was precisely determined by the
bone-rank system.

higher your status, of course, the more beautiful and higher quality these items became.

Those of true-bone rank were allowed to live in houses up to 24 *ja* (Korean feet) long or wide; for those of six-, five- and four-head rank, these dimensions shrank to 21, 18 and 15 *ja*, respectively. Meanwhile, those of six-, five- and four-head rank were allowed up to five, three or two horses in their stables. In today's terms, it would be like making a law stipulating different sizes of apartment and parking space for each person, according to social status. How about that?

Disaffection among those of six-head rank

The bone-rank system dominated the people of Silla, its influence extending from family life to wider society. Silla is sometimes even referred to as a "bone-rank society."

Naturally, those born without high hereditary status were unsatisfied. No matter how great their talent, those of six-head rank were never able to escape the shadow of the true-bone rank above them.

This is why many men of six-head rank gave up the pursuit of government positions altogether, becoming monks, scholars, or unofficial royal advisors. Wonhyo, a famous monk of whom you may have heard, was also of six-head rank. So was renowned Silla scholar Choe Chiwon.

The Three Choes of Silla
Many Silla men of six-head rank passed the *bingongke* examination. Among them were Choe Chiwon, Choe Eonwi and Choe Seungu, known collectively as the "Three Choes of Silla." Surprisingly enough, all three of them lived in the same period. Subsequently, when Silla became divided into the Later Three Kingdoms, Choe Seungu went to Later Baekje and became an informal advisor to its leader, Gyeonhwon. Choe Eonwi went to Goryeo and became a retainer to Wang Geon. Choe Chiwon, as we have seen, turned his back on the world after failing to reform Silla. Such were the different paths followed by the Three Choes of Silla. Which one would you have taken?

Choe had a reputation as a prodigy from a very young age. When he was eighteen, he went to study in Tang and passed the *bingongke*, a state examination for foreign scholars.

Sangseojang, Gyeongju
Sangseojang was used as a place of study by Choe Chiwon - maybe this is where he wrote his petition. In fact, its name means "house where a petition to the king was written." The building in this photo is a recent reconstruction.

All that awaited Choe on his return to Silla when he had finished his studies, however, was the chaos of politics and the barriers presented by the bone-rank system. He therefore petitioned the king, proposing a plan for far-reaching reforms. But his ideas were not implemented. Filled with despair, Choe abandoned his government position and spent the rest of his life drifting around the country.

Why only Silla had queens

Silla had three queens: Seondeok, Jindeok and Jinseong. In fact, it is the only state in Korean history to have had female monarchs. Why was this? Were the women of Silla particularly strong?

There were several occasions in the Goryeo and Joseon periods when women ruled the country, too. This happened at times such as when the king was too young or unable to fulfil the role of a monarch for some other reason, so that the queen consort of the deceased king, the most senior member of the royal family, would temporarily take over the political reins. This practice was known as "regency by the queen mother" and was different from the practice in Silla, where queens were proper monarchs.

The fact that Silla had queens is related to the bone-rank system. Queen Seondeok was the eldest daughter of King Jinpyeong, who had no sons. As such, Seondeok was the only individual of sacred-bone rank eligible to take the throne.

Seondeok's successor, Jindeok, also became queen in the absence of a male of sacred-bone rank. Jindeok was

Hyecho's Indian travelogue, 'Wang ocheonchukguk jeon'

In 1908, a dog-eared old book was discovered in a cave at Dunhuang in China's Gansu Province. Missing both its beginning and end parts, it was a hand-copied account of a journey to India, titled *Wang ocheonchukguk jeon* ("Memoirs of a Pilgrimage to the Five Indian Kingdoms") and written by Hyecho, a Silla monk during the reign of King Seongdeok. At the age of twenty, Hyecho travelled to Tang, where he met the Indian monk Vajrabodhi, became his disciple and sailed to India. Cheonchuk was a name used at the time for India, or for the direction in which it lay. It is said to derive from the Sanskrit word "Sindhu." Hyecho spent some four years walking through India and several Central Asian countries, making detailed records of the societies, natural environments, customs, cultures and histories he encountered. *Wang ocheonguk jeon* is a very valuable source of information about these regions in the early eighth century.

Seondeok's first cousin. Her case of Queen Jinseong was a bit more complicated: to put it simply, she was crowned in order to prevent the throne from passing into the hands of another family.

So the reason Silla had queens was not that its women were particularly free or strong, but that sometimes the search for an eligible individual according to the bone-rank system resulted in the crowning of a woman.

Silla at its peak

Silla reached its zenith around the middle of the eighth century, some 100 years after unification. At this time, it was ruled by King Gyeongdeok.

Almost all of the Silla artworks we know today were created during Gyeongdeok's reign - Bulguksa Temple;

The Divine Bell of King Seongdeok
Measuring 3.36 meters in height, 2.27 meters wide at its mouth, 7.73 meters around its rim, 24 centimeters thick and 18.9 tonnes in weight, this enormous bell took 120,000 *geun* of copper to found. There is also a legend that a baby was thrown into the molten metal.

Bulguksa Temple
This temple represents the peak of Silla culture. It was built, together with Seokguram Grotto, at the time of King Gyeongdeok.

Seokguram Grotto; the Divine Bell of King Seongdeok, better known as the "Emille Bell;" the bell at Hwangnyongsa Temple, which weighed a whopping 490,000 geun; the statue of Bhaisajyaguru (the "Medicine Buddha") at Bunhwangsa Temple, which weighed 300,000 geun; and Mt. Manbulsan, the artificial mountain with 10,000 Buddha statues admired even by the Emperor of Tang.

At its peak, Silla enjoyed political stability, and prosperity thanks to its well-developed agriculture, commerce and manufacturing. Big markets appeared in its capital, Geumseong (today's Gyeongju), and the country's culture flourished spectacularly.

The defining feature of Silla culture at this time was the way it combined its own unique aspects with the cultures

of Goguryeo, Baekje and even Tang. The framework for what we now know as Korean culture was formed in Silla.

Have you heard the legend of the Emille Bell, which tells of how a baby was thrown into the molten metal before casting? This enormous bell was founded during the reign of King Gyeongdeok, in honor of his father, Seongdeok. Its formal name is the "Divine Bell of King Seongdeok." Some also call it the "Bongdeoksa Bell," as it was hung at a temple of the same name.

The Divine Bell of King Seongdeok is a masterpiece that shows us just how outstanding the bell founding technology of Silla really was. The story about how a baby was thrown into the molten metal, however, illustrates what hardship the common people went through whenever the state founded a bell, or undertook large-scale construction work like the building of a palace or fortress. With every project, commoners had go out and work on the construction site or donate money. If they had no money, they might even be forced to sacrifice their own babies.

Silla's printing technology was brilliant, too. A copy of *Mugu jeonggwang daedarani gyeong* ("Pure Light Dharani Sutra") discovered in a pagoda at Bulguksa Temple is known to be

Clay figurine with luggage
This figurine is carrying a load almost as big as itself on its back. Is this what life was like for commoners in Silla?
−Gyeongju National Museum

the world's oldest surviving woodblock print.

During Silla's heyday, its capital, Geumseong, contained only houses with tiled roofs, with no thatch to be seen.

When cooking, the capital's residents used not wood but charcoal, which was much more expensive. This just goes to show how well off they were - understandable, since everyone living in Geumseong was either part of the nobility or very wealthy.

The story was different for ordinary commoners in the provinces, however. In years when farming went badly and the harvest was poor, some starved to death or even sold their own babies.

Hyangdeuk, who lived in Gongju, Chungcheong-do Province during the reign of King Gyeongdeok, cut off part of the flesh on his leg and fed it to his starving father at a time of famine.

Meanwhile, Sonsun, who lived during the reign of King Heungdeog, found a bell in the ground while digging a grave in which to bury alive a child who had stolen and eaten his elderly mother's meal. Thanks to his discovery, he received a house and food from the government, escaping poverty.

Stories like this show how Silla's dazzling culture concealed the grinding poverty and heart-rending struggles of its commoners.

Hyangga: songs of Silla

Hyangga were songs written and sung by the people of Silla, infused with their thoughts and feelings. At this time, Hangeul had not yet been invented and Korea therefore had no script of its own. *Hyangga* were written down using the sounds and meanings of Chinese characters.

One of the best-known *hyangga* is *Heonhwaga*, a song devoted to Lady Suro, the mother-in-law of King Gyeongdeok. Suro was extraordinarily beautiful. One day, Lady Suro was following her husband to Gangneung and had stopped by the sea to rest and eat lunch. Up on the side of a nearby cliff, she saw a gorgeous bunch of red azaleas growing. She really wanted the azaleas for herself, but nobody dared to climb the sheer cliff and pick them.

Then, an old man leading his cow past put down the rope, clambered up the cliff, picked the azaleas and gave them to Lady Suro. As he did so he improvised a song, which is now known as *Heonhwaga*.

Letting go of the cow, I climb the red cliffs.
If you'll only let me, I'll pick this flower and hand it to you.

Other *hyangga* that have survived to reach us today include *Dosolga*, *Jemangmaega*, *Changiparangga* and *Hyeseongga*. Queen Jinseong ordered her retainers to collect the *hyangga* of Silla and compile them into an anthology, titled *Samdaemok*. Unfortunately, this collection no longer survives.

Sculpture of fairy playing an instrument, discovered in Anapji Pond
– Gyeongju National Museum

CHAPTER 13

Balhae, land of mystery

In credentials sent abroad, King Mun of Balhae described himself as the "King of Goryeo" - in this instance, a reference to Goguryeo.

A message sent from Japan to Balhae, meanwhile, addresses its leader as the "King of Goryeo." And the Japanese historical text *Shoku nihongi* ("Chronicle of Japan, Continued") records an envoy sent from Balhae as having been sent from "Goryeo." The kings of Balhae regarded themselves as the successors to those of Goguryeo, and were recognized as such by other states at the time.

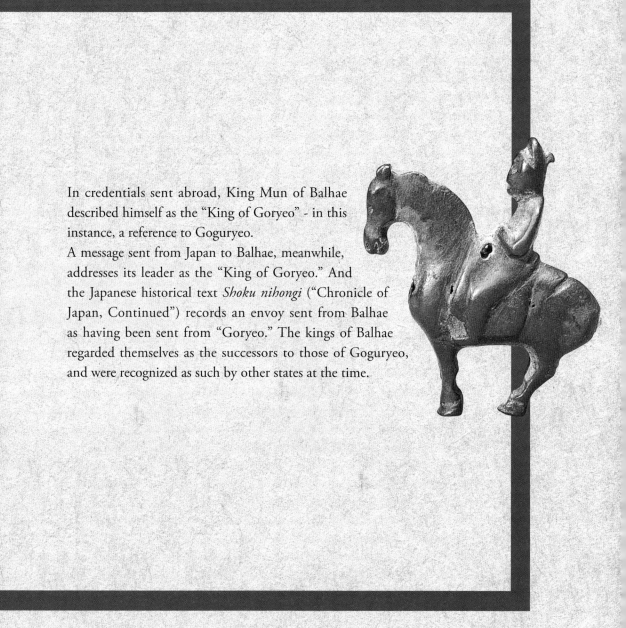

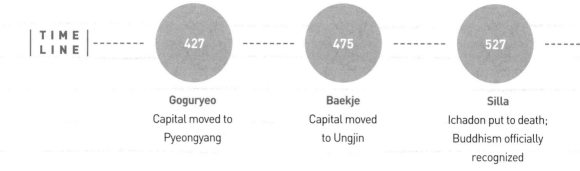

TIME LINE

427

Goguryeo
Capital moved to
Pyeongyang

475

Baekje
Capital moved
to Ungjin

527

Silla
Ichadon put to death;
Buddhism officially
recognized

Balhae was a state that appeared on the territory formerly occupied by Goguryeo, once the latter had fallen. Its existence was forgotten, however, for a long time by later Koreans, regarded as not particularly relevant to their history.

Confucian scholars in Joseon believed their state to be the latest in a lineage that ran from the Three Kingdoms through unified Silla and Goryeo. This is why they didn't consider Balhae part of their history. In the late Joseon period, however, a Silhak scholar named Yu Deukgong wrote a book called Balhae-go *("Study of Balhae"), which claimed that this part of Korean history should be referred to as the "Southern and Northern Kingdoms" period. In other words, Yu claimed, Balhae was undoubtedly part of Korean history and deserved to be considered the northern of two formerly coexisting states, the other being Silla to the south.*

Today, Balhae is widely regarded as part of Korean history. You'll find it has its own ample presence in Korean history textbooks. It remains an enigma to us, however: there are so many things we still don't know about it.

Today, I'd like to go on a journey in search of clues that might help unveil the shroud of mystery that surrounds Balhae.

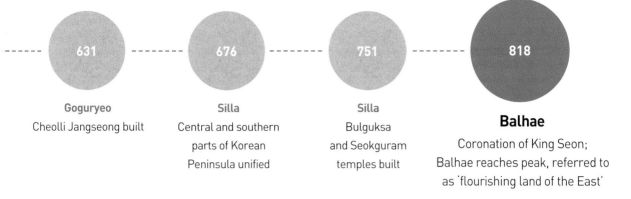

631

Goguryeo
Cheolli Jangseong built

676

Silla
Central and southern
parts of Korean
Peninsula unified

751

Silla
Bulguksa
and Seokguram
temples built

818

Balhae
Coronation of King Seon;
Balhae reaches peak, referred to
as 'flourishing land of the East'

Balhae consisted of a Mohe majority ruled by a former Goguryeo minority. The proportion is thought to have been around forty percent Goguryeo people to sixty percent Mohe, though we have no way of knowing precisely.

Doesn't this mean it's wrong to regard Balhae as Goguryeo's successor? Wouldn't it be correct to call it a Mohe state? This is, indeed, what Russian and Chinese scholars claim.

Why Balhae is part of Korean history

Who, then, are the Mohe people? Their name was given to them by the Chinese; we cannot know what they actually called themselves. The Chinese used Mohe as an umbrella name to refer to all the peoples scattered across the vast

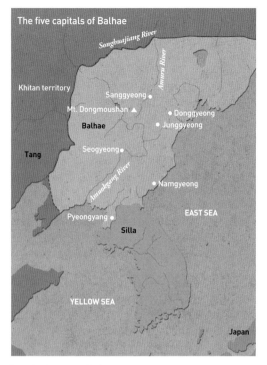

The five capitals of Balhae

In order to govern its large territory, Balhae established five capitals: Sanggyeong, Junggyeong, Donggyeong, Seogyeong and Namgyeong. Its main capital was relocated several times but remained in Sanggyeong for the longest period.

Manchuria region. The Mohe were divided into tribes such as the Somu, the Baishan, the Boduo and the Heishui. The Sumo Mohe lived near the Songhuajiang River, the Baishan in the region of Mt. Baekdusan, the Boduo to the north of the Sumo, and the Heishui near the Amur River.

In fact, however, most of the tribes called Mohe by the Chinese were former people of Goguryeo, a state that originally comprised not only ethnic Koreans but several other peoples, including Mohe and Khitan. Just as the United States today includes people of white, black and Asian races.

After the fall of Goguryeo, these people carried on living where they were. Which means that among the former people of Goguryeo were not only ethnic Koreans but Mohe-Goguryeo and Khitan-Goguryeo people, who became citizens of Balhae.

Goguryeo gilt-bronze plate used in Balhae
This plate was discovered at Jeolgol in Ome-ri, Sinpo, Hamgyeongnam-do Province. Funnily enough, despite having been discovered at a Balhae historical site, it was made in Goguryeo. This is probably because Goguryeo items were still used in Balhae.

This becomes even clearer when we learn how the people of Balhae regarded themselves. In credentials sent abroad, King Mun of Balhae described himself as the "King of Goryeo" - in this instance, a reference to Goguryeo.

A message sent from Japan to Balhae, meanwhile, addresses its leaders as the "King of Goryeo." And *Shoku nihongi* ("Chronicle of Japan, Continued"), a Japanese historical text completed in the late-eighth century, records an envoy sent from Balhae as having been sent from "Goryeo." The kings of Balhae regarded themselves as the successors to those of Goguryeo, and were recognized as such by other states at the time.

The Silla scholar Choe Chiwon understood Balhae to be the state that succeeded Goguryeo, writing, "Today's Balhae is the Goguryeo of yesteryear."

Dae Joyeong, founder of Balhae

Now let's have a look at how Balhae was founded. Remember how I told you that, after the fall of Goguryeo, 200,000 of its former citizens were taken off to Tang? These people scattered to and settled in various parts of the Chinese empire. A large number of them lived in a place called Yingzhou in Liaoxi, a region to the west of the Liaohe River, alongside Khitan and Mohe people.

Japanese wooden tablets with records of Balhae
Wooden tablets such as these, discovered at the site of a former palace in Japan, were used instead of paper at a time when the latter was very expensive. The one on the far right reads, in Chinese characters, *"gyeon goryeosa."* *Goryeosa* was the name used in Japan for envoys sent to Balhae.

Dae Joyeong was a Goguryeo man who lived in Yingzhou. Eventually, the Khitan inhabitants of Yingzhou staged a revolt in protest at the extreme abuse of non-Tang nationals by local governor Zhao Wenhui. Ethnic Goguryeo and Mohe people also joined in the uprising, led by Geolsa Biu of the Mohe and by Dae Joyeong's father, Geolgeol Jungsang. Tang sent troops to quell the revolt, but they achieved little.

Seizing an opportunity, Geolsa Biu and Geolgeol Jungsang escaped Yingzhou and headed east. Tang sent General Li Kaigu after them and Geolsa Biu ended up dying in battle when his troops met those of Tang.

The surviving Mohe and Goguryeo people fought a final battle with Tang forces at Tianmenling, a densely forested and highly rugged area in Jilin, Manchuria. Dae Joyeong had his troops lie in wait in the woods for the Tang troops, which they then wiped out in an ambush.

Dae Joyeong led his remaining followers across the Songhuajiang River to Mt. Dongmoushan, a mountain known today as Chengshanzi Mountain Fortress in Dunhua, in Manchuria's Jilin Province - former Goguryeo territory. He built a palace and a fortress at the foot of Mt. Dongmoushan, founded a new state and made the fortress its capital. He called the country "Jin." It was 698, exactly thirty years after the fall of Goguryeo's Pyeongyangseong Fortress.

Balhae: 'flourishing land of the East'

Jin grew at a dazzling pace. It sent envoys to the Turkic Khaganate and Silla and established amicable relations with both, while gradually growing in strength as it acquired one piece of former Goguryeo territory after another. Emperor Xianzong of Tang had no choice but to send an envoy of his own and ask for reconciliation, addressing Dae Joyeong as "King of Balhae." Tang, in other words, recognized Jin. It was from this moment on that Jin came to be called "Balhae."

After Dae Joyeong's death, crown prince Muye took the throne and became King Mu. The new monarch maintained close ties to Japan while fighting Tang. Silla, despite initially trying to stay on good terms with Balhae, allied with Tang as its northern neighbor rapidly gained strength.

King Mun, Mu's successor, ended Balhae's conflict with Tang, established close relations with it and concentrated on internal affairs. He moved his country's capital from Dongmoushan to Shangjing Longquanfu by the Mudanjiang

Column base stones from a corridor at Sanggyeongseong Fortress
These column foundation stones indicate the former location of a palace corridor. Sangyeongseong was home to no less than seven palaces, which gives you some idea of how splendid it must have been.

Stone lion found at a Sanggyeongseong palace site
This forbidding expression was meant to guard the palace.

Balhae stone lantern
At 6.4 meters tall, this huge stone lantern is around the same height as the Gwanggaeto Stele. It stands on the site of a Buddhist temple in the old Bahae capital, Sanggyeong. If the stone lantern is this big, we can only guess how majestic the temple itself must have been.

River. This place is now known as Dongjingcheng and located in Ning'an in Heilongjiang Province, Manchuria.

Balhae reached its peak in the early ninth century, around 150 years after it was founded. After embracing the cultures of Goguryeo and Tang, it had developed a unique culture of its own. It also adopted cultural traits from the Turkic Khaganate and other Central Asian states. The splendor of Balhae culture reached its apogee around the ninth century, under the rule of King Seon.

Balhae spread as far as its border with Silla to the south, the Amur River to the north, the sea to the east and Khitan territory to the west. Most of today's North Korea, Manchuria and Russia's Primorsky Krai was Balhae territory. Tang called the northern Korean state "flourishing land of the East."

Two mystery-solving princesses

It was thanks to two princesses that we finally came to know what Balhae, which had remained an enigma for so long, was like. When the tombs of princesses Jeonghye and Jeonghyo, the second and fourth daughters of King Mun, were discovered, the various artifacts, murals and epitaphs they contained answered many questions about the mysterious state.

The two princesses died young, before their father. King

Murals in the tomb of Princess Jeonghyo
These murals depict twelve warriors and musicians and are highly valuable for the knowledge they give us about the people of Balhae. Some scholars claim that the twelve figures, though dressed as men, are in fact women in disguise and that it was fashionable in Balhae for women to dress as men.

Mun appears to have loved them deeply, to the extent where their deaths left him so sad that he was barely able to concentrate on ruling the country.

The tomb of Princess Jeonghyo contains a mural depicting twelve people. They appear to have been figures that served the princess: warriors guarding the gate of a huge mansion, maids in waiting, musicians playing, servants holding parasols to provide shade...

The figures in these murals allow us a guess at what the people of Balhae looked like. Their faces are plump, with round cheeks, and they appear to have been well fed.

The epitaphs in the two tombs were the first discovered examples of anything written in Chinese characters by Balhae people. Their contents teach us a lot about the country.

The inscriptions indicate that Chinese learning in Balhae

reached quite a high level. Like Silla, Balhae sent scholars to study in Tang, several of whom passed the *bingongke* examination.

Silla and Balhae students sent to Tang competed with each other in their studies for the glory of their respective countries.

Balhae was a Buddhist country, having inherited the faith from Goguryeo. A wonderful energy flows through its Buddhist artworks, which include beautiful Buddha statues, stone lanterns and roof tiles with lotus patterns.

Balhae roof tiles were well-made and highly durable. Many of them feature inscriptions, some in Chinese characters but others in an unrecognizable script. Could this mean that Balhae had its own writing system?

Among the country's finest products were its horses and sable pelts. Go Jedeok, a Balhae envoy who sailed across the East Sea to Japan to establish ties between the two countries, took 300 sable pelts with him.

The fall of Balhae

Balhae lasted for around 230 years. Even as Silla split into the Later Three Kingdoms and Gungye, Gyeonhwon and Wang

Site of Sanggyeongseong Fortress
This aerial photograph shows the square outline of the site of Sanggyeongseong Fortress. Balhae was the largest Korean state in history, but its former territory is now divided among three countries: China, Russia and North Korea. Studying the history of Balhae is hard without the cooperation of these three countries.

Geon fought fiercely among themselves, Balhae remained proud and strong to their north. So why did this powerful state eventually fall?

Balhae was brought down by the Khitan. Having expanded eastwards from the grassy plains of Mongolia, they eventually became a threat. In 926, they laid siege to the Balhae capital, Sanggyeong. Its last king, Dae Inseon, surrendered in a matter of days.

How did such a powerful state collapse like this? There are no surviving history books written by its people, so we cannot know for sure, but a Khitan historical text describes how "We took advantage of internal discord in Balhae and defeated it without a fight." Perhaps, then, Balhae collapsed in the face of the Khitan attack after being

Gilt-bronze figurine on horseback
Discovered at the former site of Sanggyeong, this figurine is now in Japan.

weakened, like Goguryeo before it, by power struggles within its ruling classes.

So what became of the surviving former citizens of Balhae? Dae Gwanghyeon, the country's last crown prince, fled to Goryeo where he was treated with generosity by Wang Geon. Many other former Balhae citizens followed suit.

Yeonggwangtap Pagoda
There may be a tomb below this pagoda: building pagodas above tombs was a unique Balhae custom.

 Balhae poetry

The poems in classical Chinese left by Balhae envoys to Japan offer us some idea of their mastery of this language. When envoys arrived from Balhae, the Japanese picked their best Chinese language experts to receive them.

The following is a poem by Wang Hyoryeom, a Balhae man dispatched as an envoy in 814. Written in classical Chinese, it appears to reflect Wang's delight with the kind hospitality offered him:

At this feast you have put on for us
People are as merry as they get back in Sanggyeong.
It seems even the rain understands,
Showering its affection down on this weary traveller.

Balhae's road network

Balhae's central government consisted of three chancelleries and six ministries. It ruled the rest of its territory by dividing it into five capitals, fifteen provinces and sixty-two counties. The five capitals were named Sanggyeong, Donggyeong, Seogyeong, Namgyeong and Junggyeong. Sanggyeong was a large city, modelled after the Tang capital Chang'an; a long, straight road, called Jujak, ran through its center.

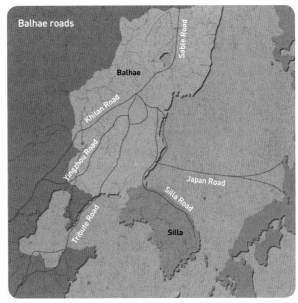

Balhae's territory was extremely extensive - at its peak, it may have been even larger than Goguryeo. Good roads were needed if such a large territory was to be governed. Just as the Romans built roads from conquered lands to their capital in order to govern them more effectively, giving rise to the expression, "all roads lead to Rome," Balhae built routes of its own for the same purpose.

There were roads linking the five capitals, a road to Tang via Yeongju-do and Jogong-do, a road to Khitan territory, a sea route to Japan, a road to Silla, and the "Sable Road," which led to Siberia and Central Asia. "All roads led to Sanggyeong," you might say...

Sanggyeong's markets were full of goods from all regions - there was nothing that couldn't be found there. Such abundance was thanks to the trade enabled by Balhae's network of good roads.

Index

Museum

Picture

Map

Bibliography

Historical records and books ─────────

김부식(金富軾),《삼국사기(三國史記)》

일연(一然),《삼국유사(三國遺事)》

진수(陳壽),《삼국지 위서 오환선비동이전(三國志魏書烏丸鮮卑東夷傳)》

이규보(李奎報),《동명왕편(東明王篇)》

각훈(覺訓) 외,《해동고승전(海東高僧傳) 외》, 동국역경원, 1994

전용신 역,《일본서기(日本書紀)》, 일지사, 1989

김대문(金大問), 이종욱 역주해,《화랑세기(花郎世記)》, 소나무, 1999

혜초(慧超), 이석호 역,《왕오천축국전(往五天竺國傳) 외》, 을유문화사, 1993

유득공(柳得恭), 송기호 옮김,《발해고(渤海考)》, 홍익출판사, 2000

한국고전번역원 www.itkc.or.kr

John D. Barrow, *THE ORIGIN OF THE UIVERSE*, Brockman, Inc., New York. NY., 1994, 최승언.이은아 옮김,《우주의 기원》, 동아출판사, 1995

Richard Dawkins, *RIVER OUT OF EDEN*, Brockman, Inc. New York. NY., 1994, 이용철 옮김,《에덴 밖의 강》, 동아출판사, 1995

Ernst Mayr, *WHAT EVOLUTION IS*, Brockman, Inc., New York. NY., 2001, 임지원 옮김,《진화란 무엇인가》, 사이언스북스, 2008

Richard Leakey, *THE ORIGIN OF HUMANKIND*, Brockman, Inc. New York. NY., 1994, 황현숙 역,《인류의 기원》, 동아출판사, 1995

Richard Leakey and Roger Lewin, *ORIGINS RECONSIDERED*, John Brockman Associates, Inc., 1992, 최정필 옮김,《속 오리진》, 세종서적, 1995

Donald C. Johanson.Maitland A. Edey, *LUCY, THE BEGINNINGS OF HUMANKIND*, Simon and Schuster, New York, 1981, 이충호 역,《최초의 인간 루시》, 푸른숲, 1996

Clive Ponting, *THE GREEN HISTORY OF THE WORLD*, Penguin Books Ltd, 1992, 이진아 역,《녹색세계사 1-2》, 심지, 1995

Jared Diamond, *GUNS, GERMS, AND STEEL*, c/o Brockman, Inc., New York, 1997, 김진준 옮김,《총, 균, 쇠》, 문학사상사, 2005

Jared Diamond, *THE THIRD CHIMPANZEE*, Brockman, Inc., New York, NY., 1993, 김정흠 옮김,《제3의 침팬지》, 문학사상사, 1996

William H. McNeill, *A World History*, Oxford University Press, 1999, 김우영 옮김,《세계의 역사》1, 이산, 2007

이형구,《한국 고대문화의 기원》, 까치, 1991

이형구 엮음,《단군과 고조선》, 살림터, 1999

노태돈 외,《단군과 고조선사》, 사계절, 2000

송호정,《한국 고대사 속의 고조선사》, 푸른역사, 2003

송호정,《단군, 만들어진 신화》, 산처럼, 2004

윤내현,《고조선연구》, 일지사, 1994

이영문,《고인돌 이야기》, 다지리, 2001

이영문,《한국 지석묘 사회 연구》, 학연문화사, 2002

최몽룡.김선우 편저,《한국 지석묘 연구 이론과 방법》, 주류성, 2000

석광준,《조선의 고인돌 무덤 연구》, 중심, 2002

하문식,《고조선 지역의 고인돌 연구》, 백산자료원, 1999

이현혜,《삼한사회 형성과정 연구》, 일조각, 1984

한국고대사연구회 편,《삼한의 사회와 문화》, 신서원, 1995

이필영,《솟대》, 대원사, 1990

김두진,《한국 고대의 건국신화와 제의》, 일조각, 1999

최광식,《고대 한국의 국가와 제사》, 한길사, 1994

김기흥,《고구려 건국사》, 창작과비평사, 2002

김태식,《가야연맹사》, 일조각, 1993

김태식,《미완의 문명 7백년 가야사》1-3, 푸른역사, 2002

고준환,《신비 왕국 가야》, 우리출판사, 1993

부산대학교 한국민족문화연구소 편,《한국 고대사 속의 가야》,

혜안, 2001

한국고대학회, 《가야사의 제문제》, 한국고대학회 제3회 학술발
　표회 자료집, 1992

노태돈, 《고구려사 연구》, 사계절, 1999

전호태, 《고구려 고분벽화 연구》, 사계절, 2000

김용만, 《고구려의 발견》, 바다출판사, 1998

이진희, 이기동 역, 《광개토왕릉 비(碑)의 탐구》, 일조각, 1982

김현구, 《임나일본부연구》, 일조각, 1993

이기동, 《백제사연구》, 일조각, 1996

이도학, 《새로 쓰는 백제사》, 푸른역사, 1997

김성호, 《비류백제와 일본의 국가기원》, 지문사, 1982

나경수, 《마한 신화》, 한얼미디어, 2004

나경수.서해숙, 《서동요》, 한얼미디어, 2005

최광식, 《한국 고대의 토착신앙과 불교》, 고려대출판부, 1999

임동권, 《일본 안의 백제문화》, 규장각, 1996

홍윤기, 《한국인이 만든 일본 국보》, 문학세계사, 1995

박천수, 《새로 쓰는 고대 한일교섭사》, 사회평론, 2007

이성우, 《동아시아 속의 고대 한국 식생활사 연구》, 향문사, 1992

김용만, 《새로 쓰는 연개소문 전(傳)》, 바다출판사, 2003

김기흥, 《천년의 왕국 신라》, 창작과비평사, 2000

이종욱, 《신라 골품제 연구》, 일조각, 1999

이종욱, 《화랑세기로 본 신라인 이야기》, 김영사, 2000

이기동, 《신라 사회사 연구》, 일조각, 1997

무함마드 깐수, 《신라.서역 교류사》, 단국대학교출판부, 1992

조범환, 《우리 역사의 여왕들》, 책세상, 2000

송기호, 《발해를 찾아서-만주 연해주 답사기》, 솔, 1993

송기호, 《발해정치사연구》, 일조각, 1995

방학봉, 《발해문화연구》, 이론과실천, 1991

이성시, 김창석 역, 《동아시아의 왕권과 교역-신라.발해와 정창
　원 보물》, 청년사, 1999

정진헌, 《실학자 유득공의 고대사 인식》, 신서원, 1998

국사편찬위원회, 《한국사》 2-10, 1995-1998

강만길 외, 《한국사》 1-4, 한길사, 1995

이기백 외, 《한국고대사론》, 한길사, 1988

이기백, 《한국고대 정치사회사연구》, 일조각, 1996

김기흥, 《새롭게 쓴 한국고대사》, 역사비평사, 1993

신채호, 《조선상고사》 상.하, 삼성문화문고 99,100, 1977

한국역사연구회, 《삼국시대 사람들은 어떻게 살았을까》, 청년사,
　1998

이이화, 《한국사 이야기》 1-4, 한길사, 1998

젊은역사연구모임, 《영화처럼 읽는 한국사》, 1999

한국생활사박물관 편찬위원회, 《한국생활사박물관》 1-6, 사계
　절, 2000~2002

전국역사교사모임, 《살아있는 한국사 교과서》 1, 휴머니스트,
　2002

이야기 한국역사 편집위원회, 《이야기 한국역사》 1-3, 풀빛,
　1997

이기백, 《신수판(新修版) 한국사신론》, 일조각, 1994

변태섭, 《한국사 통론(通論)》, 삼영사, 1986

한국역사연구회, 《한국역사》, 역사비평사, 1992

한국사특강편찬위원회 편, 《한국사 특강》, 서울대학교 출판부,
　1990

한국역사연구회, 《한국사강의》, 한울아카데미, 1989

역사문제연구소, 《사진과 그림으로 보는 한국의 역사》 1, 웅진닷
　컴, 1993

박한용.장원정.황경, 《시와 이야기가 있는 우리 역사》 1, 동녘,
　1996

구로 역사연구소, 《바로 보는 우리 역사》 1, 거름, 1990

한국민중사연구회 편, 《한국민중사》 1, 풀빛, 1986

신복룡, 《한국사 새로 보기》, 풀빛, 2001

박은봉, 《한국사 상식 바로잡기》, 책과함께, 2007

박은봉, 《한권으로 보는 한국사 100장면》, 가람기획, 1993/《한국
　사 100장면》 (개정판), 실천문학사, 1997

박은봉, 《한권으로 보는 세계사 100장면》, 가람기획, 1992/《세계
　사 100장면》 (개정판), 실천문학사, 1996

박은봉, 《한국사 뒷이야기》, 실천문학사, 1997

박은봉, 《세계사 뒷이야기》, 실천문학사, 1994

박은봉, 《엄마의 역사편지》 1, 웅진주니어, 2000

Academic papers and essays

김두진, 단군고기의 이해 방향,《한국 고대의 건국신화와 제의》, 일조각, 1999

김두진, 단군신화의 문화사적 접근,《한국 고대의 건국신화와 제의》, 일조각, 1999

이기백, 고조선의 국가형성,《한국사 시민강좌》2, 일조각, 1988

김정배, 고조선의 주민구성과 그 문화적 복합,《한국민족문화의 기원》, 고려대학교출판부, 1973

방선주, 한.중 고대 기년(紀年)의 제문제,《아시아문화》2, 1987

송호정, 고조선 국가형성과정 연구, 서울대 박사논문, 1999

지건길, 한반도 고인돌 문화의 원류와 전개,《마한백제문화》13, 1993

이융조.하문식, 한국 고인돌의 다른 유형에 관한 연구-제단고인돌 형식을 중심으로,《동방학지》63, 1989

임병태, 한국 지석묘의 형식 및 연대 문제,《사총》9, 1964

윤무병, 한국 묘제의 변천,《충남대 인문과학연구소 논문집》2-5, 1975

서영수, 고조선의 위치와 강역,《한국사 시민강좌》2, 일조각, 1988

이현혜, 동예와 옥저,《한국사 4》, 국사편찬위원회, 1997

김정배, 위지동이전에 나타난 고대인의 생활습속-장례.혼례를 중심으로,《대동문화연구》13, 1979

나희라, 신라의 국가 및 왕실 조상제사 연구, 서울대 박사논문, 1999

旗田 巍, 이기동 역, 광개토왕릉비문의 제문제,《일본인의 한국관》, 일조각, 1983

권오영, 백제국에서 백제로의 전환,《역사와 현실》40, 2001

권오영, 백제의 성립과 발전,《한국사》6, 국사편찬위원회, 1995

양기석, 한성시대 후기의 정치적 변화,《한국사》6, 국사편찬위원회, 1995

이완형, '무왕'조의 찬술의도와 서동요의 성격,《어문학》74, 2001

최광식, 이차돈 설화에 대한 신고찰,《한국전통문화연구》1, 1985

최광식, 무속신앙이 한국불교에 끼친 영향-산신각과 장승을 중심으로,《백산학보》26, 1981

최광식, 신라의 불교 전래, 수용 및 공인,《신라문화제 학술연구 발표집》12, 1991

이종철.정명섭, 의식주 생활,《한국사》8, 국사편찬위원회, 1998

신형식, 김유신 가문의 성립과 활동,《이화사학연구》13.14합집, 1983

김선주, 고구려 서옥제의 혼인형태,《고구려연구》13집, 2002

신동진, 고구려 초기의 혼인체계 분석, 건국대학교 석사논문, 1984

송기중, 언어,《한국사》8, 국사편찬위원회, 1998

박찬흥, 삼국간에 말이 통했을까?,《삼국시대 사람들은 어떻게 살았을까》, 청년사, 1998

김영하, 삼국시대 왕의 통치형태 연구, 고려대 박사논문, 1989

젊은역사연구모임, 통일을 이루지 못한 '통일신라',《영화처럼 읽는 한국사》, 1999

정용숙, 신라의 여왕들,《한국사 시민강좌》15, 1994

문경현, 시왕설(弑王設)과 선덕여왕,《백산학보》52, 1999

서의식, 신라 상대(上代)의 왕위계승과 성골,《한국사연구》86, 1994

전기웅, 신라 하대(下代) 말의 정치사회와 경문왕가家,《부산사학》16, 1989

배한극, 혜초〈왕오천축국전〉의 세계사적 의의,《역사교육논집》40, 2008

유영봉,〈왕오천축국전〉연구,《고려 문학의 탐색》, 이회문화사, 2001

홍기삼, 수로부인,《향가설화문학》, 민음사, 1997

송기호, 발해의 문화와 발해사 인식의 변천,《한국사》10, 국사편찬위원회, 1996

한규철, 발해국의 주민구성,《한국사학보》, 1996 창간호

젊은역사연구모임, 발해사는 누구의 역사인가,《영화처럼 읽는 한국사》, 1999

김종복, 발해 폐왕.성왕대 정치세력의 동향,《역사와 현실》41, 2001

방학봉, 정혜공주묘와 정효공주묘에 대하여,《발해사연구》1, 연변대학출판사, 1990

From prehistory to Unified Silla and Balhae

Letters from Korean History

Volume I

First Published 5 May 2016
Fourth Published 10 April 2023

Author | Park Eunbong
Translator | Ben Jackson
Illustrator | Illustration; Ryu Dongpil, Map; Yu Sanghyeon

Design | Lee Seokwoon, Kim Miyeon

Published by | Cum Libro Inc. **CUM LIBRO 책과함께**
Address | 2F, Sowaso Bldg. 70, Donggyo-ro, Mapo-gu, Seoul, Korea 04022
Tel | (+82) 2-335-1982
Fax | (+82) 2-335-1316
E-mail | prpub@daum.net
Blog | blog.naver.com/prpub
Registered | 3 April 2003 No. 25100-2003-392

ISBN 979-11-86293-48-5 04740
ISBN 979-11-86293-46-1 (set)